Courageous Enough to Laugh

Joy in the Midst of Storms

Written by Dr. Nandi Louise

COURAGEOUS ENOUGH TO LAUGH
JOY IN THE MIDST OF STORMS
By Dr. Nandi Louise
Published by Thrive Revolution Publishing
Daytona Beach, Florida

Copyright © 2025 – Dr. Nandi Louise
Herndon, VA 20171
www.nandilouise.com

All rights reserved. This book is protected by the copyright laws of the United States of America. No part of this book may be reprinted for commercial gain or profit or reproduced in any form by any electronic or mechanical means including photocopying, recording or information storage and retrieval without permission in writing. The use of quotations or occasional page copying for personal, or group study is permitted and encouraged. Permission will be granted upon request.

Photographs by jackiehicksportraitartist.com
Cover design by Ese Gift 31Designs
Editing by Marcie Wright

Soft cover ISBN: 978-0-578-59843-7
Hard cover ISBN: 979-8-9895655-8-0
Audiobook ISBN: 979-8-9895655-7-3
Library of Congress Control Number: 2025920196

Scripture quotations are taken from various translations and are clearly marked throughout the text. Scripture quotations marked (KJV) are from the King James Version, which is in the public domain. Scripture quotations marked (NKJV) are taken from the New King James Version®. Copyright © 1982 by Thomas Nelson. Used by permission. All rights reserved. Scripture quotations marked (NLT) are taken from the Holy Bible, New Living Translation. Copyright © 1996, 2004, 2015 by Tyndale House Foundation. Used by permission of Tyndale House Publishers, Inc., Carol Stream, Illinois 60188. All rights reserved. Scripture quotations marked (NIV) are taken from the Holy Bible, New International Version®. Copyright © 1973, 1978, 1984, 2011 by Biblica, Inc.® Used by permission of Zondervan. All rights reserved worldwide. Scripture quotations marked (AMP) are taken from the Amplified® Bible. Copyright © 1954, 1958, 1962, 1964, 1965, 1987 by The Lockman Foundation. Used by permission. www.Lockman.org. Scripture quotations marked (MSG) are taken from The Message. Copyright © 1993–2002 by Eugene H. Peterson. Used by permission of NavPress. All rights reserved. Represented by Tyndale House Publishers, Inc. Scripture quotations marked (ERV) are taken from the Holy Bible: Easy-to-Read Version™. Copyright © 1987, 1999, 2006 by Bible League International. Used by permission. All rights reserved. www.BibleLeague.org. Scripture quotations taken from The Voice™ are Copyright © 2012 by Ecclesia Bible Society. Used by permission. All rights reserved. Scripture quotations marked (TPT) are from The Passion Translation®. Copyright © 2017, 2018, 2020 by Passion & Fire Ministries, Inc. Used by permission. All rights reserved. www.ThePassionTranslation.com.

Printed in the United States of America

Dedication

To my beautiful mother, Sonja Wilson, who has gone to be with the Lord:
I love and miss you very much. You ensured that I was the strongest, feistiest powerhouse in the world. You would be proud of the laughter in this book.

To my natural father, Harry Wilson, who is not here with me anymore:
You were the funniest person — a remarkable storyteller with a gift for making others laugh. You left me a legacy of laughter that I will carry to the ends of the earth.

To my Father, God:
Without Your love, joy, peace, patience, kindness, goodness, faithfulness, and self-control, I don't know where I would be.
Thank You for every time You woke me up to laugh, even when I didn't feel like laughing; for holding me tight, hugging me, and planting precious kisses on my forehead; for understanding my moments of doubt and teaching me to trust; for guiding me in Your pathways that drip with

abundance — leading me into unstoppable growth and prosperity.

Thank You for loving me for who I am when others wanted me to diminish my personality.

Thank You for every encounter, every encouragement, every transformation, every healing, and every moment of unspeakable joy.

Thank You for dancing with me, and for putting up with my singing.

Thank You for every creative dream and idea we have shared together.

I dedicate every word, every laugh, every breakthrough to You.

Acknowledgments

To my dear friend since 9th grade, Veonca:
Thank you for opening your home to me when I was a young girl, giving me a safe place to take cover from joyless times and cry without questions or judgment. Your quiet kindness has stayed with me all these years, a reminder that love sometimes speaks loudest in silence.

To my sista gurls, Darlena, Tameka, Kesha, and Val:
Thank you for never letting me lose sight of my laughter, my destiny, or God's plan for my life. Your sisterhood, encouragement, and joy have been priceless treasures.

To my book coach, Aisha, and my Author Academy coach, Dr. Melanie:
Thank you for answering God's call on your lives and pouring your gifts into me. Your wisdom, guidance, and belief helped bring this vision from my heart to the pages of this book.

To every challenging supervisor God placed in my path:
Thank you for shaping my character and destiny. Each one of you has played a part in the story He is writing through me.

To my family, friends, co-workers, and everyone who has journeyed with me:

Thank you for being a part of my story. Whether through encouragement, laughter, prayers, or simply showing up when it mattered most, you have helped shape the woman I am today.

I carry your love and your impact with me, and I dedicate this work not just to my journey, but to the beautiful community that has walked alongside me.

Thank you for believing in the sound of laughter.
Thank you for believing in me.

Table of Contents

Foreword 12

A Testimony of Transformation 15

Defining Laughter 18

The Invitation 22

Chapter 1: The Power Behind My Laughter 28

Chapter 2: Laughter is a Calling 40

Chapter 3: Laughter is Healing 60

Chapter 4: Laughter is a Gift 74

Chapter 5: Laughter is a Weapon 84

Chapter 6: Natural Gift with Supernatural Results 111

Chapter 7: When Laughter Becomes a Message 124

Chapter 8: Her Name is Laughter: The Prophetic Power of Identity ... 132

Conclusion: But Not the End 148

Daily Dose of Laughter Confessions 158

Prayer and Declarations 170

Laughter Quotes 175

About the Author 176

Foreword

It's a rare and sacred privilege … an honor… in life to walk alongside someone not only as a friend, but as a witness to their Godly expression and gift unfolding. For over two decades, I've had the privilege of calling Nandi both a beloved friend and now a trusted colleague. Our bond has been rooted in a shared passion for soul health, deep inner healing, and helping others discover their path toward wholeness.

Over the years, I have watched Nandi receive profound revelation — what at the time seemed almost countercultural insight — into the healing power of laughter. Long before the research caught up, she was being shown by God that laughter wasn't just a response to something humorous; it was a balm, a medicine, a key to unlocking emotional, physical, and spiritual healing — just as Proverbs 17:22 says, "A merry heart does good, like medicine" (New King James Version).

In those early days, little was known in clinical or scientific circles about the biology of laughter as therapy. It was dismissed as lighthearted, even silly, but God was showing Nandi that what the world overlooked held transformational power. True to His nature, He was using what seemed as "foolish things of the world to confound the wise" (1 Corinthians 1:27, King James Version).

As Nandi journeyed with this revelation, laughter became more than an expression — it became her ministry. She began noticing how her own laughter carried a tangible shift. People — complete strangers — would approach her in grocery stores, airports, conferences, and say things like, "when you laughed, my migraine left," or ,"something in me settled when I heard you." What was happening was more than coincidence. It was sacred. God was revealing Himself through laughter.

Her laugh became a healing frequency, a divine transmission.

Recognizing the weight and wonder of what God was entrusting to her, Nandi deepened her understanding of both the spiritual and scientific dimensions of laughter. She became a certified Laughter Coach with World Laughter Tour and began merging revelation with research, spirit with science. She has since emerged as a pioneer in the field, carrying both anointing and expertise — an uncommon blend.

God also began to show her laughter as a weapon — a spiritual tool for disarming despair, breaking through trauma, and restoring joy to weary hearts. To be entrusted as a guardian of this truth is no small thing. It is a divine assignment that blesses not only the Kingdom of God but also the mental and emotional well-being of humanity.

As a Kingdom-centered psychotherapist and coach, I have the honor of walking with clients through the transformative journey of self-redesign — rebuilding identity, purpose, and emotional well-being. I vividly remember watching Nandi lead a laughter session where she invited the group to engage in intentional laughter — not driven by humor but led by choice. The shift in the atmosphere was undeniable. Lightness, release, and peace began to fill the room. That moment left a lasting impact on me. Since then, I've given clients homework assignments to "laugh on purpose." It's not about pretending — it's about choosing the medicine of laughter. Even when laughter is deliberate, it activates endorphins, reduces stress, soothes the nervous system, and gently makes space for joy to rise again.

This book is a gift. A guide. A breakthrough in its own right. Whether you are a seeker of healing, a clinician looking for tools, or a heart that simply needs to remember how to laugh again — may Nandi's journey, wisdom, and anointed joy become your invitation to deeper healing and becoming a "Laughaholic ™."

Let your heart be light.
Let your body respond.
Let your soul laugh.

With deep admiration and joy,

— **Dr. Darlena Austin, PhD, LCSW-C**
SynHerGy Behavioral Strategies
Darlenaaustin.com

A Testimony of Transformation
When Laughter Breaks Chains

Nandi Louise is an extraordinary woman of God who radiates joy with an undeniable presence. I first met her at a women's retreat several years ago, where her infectious laughter and exuberance immediately stood out. At first, I mistook her joyful nature for mere enthusiasm, as her laughter was both powerful and unrestrained. However, as we began to share testimonies of God's goodness and the supernatural power of joy, I found myself laughing just as freely, realizing that her joy was not simply a personality trait; it was a ministry.

Nandi carries a unique anointing: a ministry of laughter. She shared remarkable testimonies of individuals who experienced healing and deliverance after the Holy Spirit moved through joyful laughter. This was a concept I had never encountered before, yet as she spoke, I began to recognize the profound authority and breakthrough that joy carries in the Kingdom of God.

Sometime later, Nandi and I were both invited to speak at another retreat. During her session, she led us in a powerful exercise: she instructed each of us to recall a painful experience and, by faith, laugh at it — releasing it into God's healing presence. One by one, women stepped forward, boldly laughing over past wounds and finding freedom in the process.

However, when my turn came, I was unable to laugh. My mouth locked shut, and I felt an overwhelming sense of embarrassment. No matter how much I wanted to participate, I simply could not bring myself to release laughter.

Later, I realized that my struggle was rooted in deeply ingrained beliefs. Growing up, I had been taught that excessive laughter was a sign of carnality. I had witnessed ministers being criticized for displaying too much joy. But even beyond that, I discovered a more profound issue: I had never believed I had the right to joy or to laugh freely. My childhood had been marked by trauma, and somewhere along the way, I lost my ability to embrace pure, unrestrained joy. It wasn't just that I couldn't laugh — I had internalized the lie that I did not deserve to.

Recognizing my struggle, Nandi began to pray for me, interceding for my breakthrough. For nearly twenty minutes, we travailed in the presence of God. She demanded the enemy release my laughter and laughed at the devil for me. Her laughter was different. As she laughed over my entire body, I felt a breakthrough. I experienced the presence of God working in me. Tears flowed as she prayed for the weight of my past pain to be lifted. And then — something shifted.

I released my laughter.
And healing took place.

For the first time in years, I laughed — not a forced or polite chuckle, but genuine, Spirit-filled laughter. In that moment, I encountered the power of joy as a divine force of healing and restoration.

The joy of the Lord is our strength.
So often, we feel weary — not because we lack faith, and not because we do not love God, but because we have yet to fully embrace joy.

I wholeheartedly recommend reading *Courageous Enough to Laugh*.
Nandi's ministry carries a profound revelation that has the power to transform your understanding of joy, and bring healing to the deepest places of your heart.

— **Dr. Juanita Woodson**
Women on Fire Ministries
Juanitawoodson.com

Defining Laughter

Merriam-Webster Definition:

Laughter (noun): a sound of amusement, a response to humor or joy; an audible expression of happiness, to be of a kind that inspires joy

When God first asked me to look up the meaning of laughter, I assumed I already knew it. After all, I've been laughing all my life. But how many things do we just assume we understand — until God gives us fresh eyes? What I discovered was simple on the surface, but deeply spiritual underneath.
Laughter isn't just an amusement. It's a release. It's healing. It's a revelation.
And in this journey, it became a calling.

To laugh (*verb*):

- To show emotion (such as joy or scorn) with a chuckle or explosive sound
- To find amusement or pleasure in something
- To produce a sound that expresses mirth

Laughter (*noun*):

- The act or sound of laughing
- A spontaneous expression of joy
- A contagious form of release and healing

- To be of the kind that inspires joy

Here are just a few ways laughter shows up:
(*adjectives for the noun*)

- Loud, Soft, Boisterous, Hearty, Infectious, Uncontrollable, Explosive, Roaring, Convulsive

God's Definition of Laughter:
(*spiritually revealed meaning*)

- **Internal triumph** – a victory that starts within
- **To be whole** – complete in spirit, soul, and body
- **To be healed** – restoration from pain, sorrow, or trauma
- **Breakthrough** – a sudden shift into freedom or clarity
- **Weapon** – a divine strategy for warfare and joy

Did you know that this is what laughter really means?
Most people don't. Now that you do… everything is about to change.

You are cordially invited
to celebrate the miracle of laughter, the fragrance
of joy, and the healing presence of God.

Event: Courageous Enough to Laugh
Occasion: A Journey into Joy
Host: The Holy Spirit, with your joyful guide,
Dr. Nandi Louise
Attire: Come clothed in expectancy, hope,
and freedom
Location: Right here, between the pages of
this book
Time: Now — because healing and
laughter cannot wait

Prepare your heart.
The celebration is about to begin.

The Invitation

And Sarah said, "God has graced me with the gift of laughter! To be sure, everyone who hears my story will laugh with me.

— Genesis 21:6 (Voice)

It's party time!

This is the place to be — an event no one should miss. The guest list includes the elite and a few close friends. If you haven't figured it out by now, you are my close friends, and I'm inviting you to laugh and celebrate with me.

Tonight promises an experience unlike any other — an evening of joy so rich it will leave everyone breathless, longing for more.

Guests begin to arrive, yet the hostess is nowhere in sight. The atmosphere is captivating. Her home is elegantly adorned with wildflowers of every color, filling the air with the scent of romance.

But there's something deeper in the fragrance. It's the aroma of laughter and the scent of peace.

Close your eyes. Breathe it in.
Mmm... delightful, right!?

Warmly lit candles cast a golden glow throughout the house, their soft flicker dancing across chiffon drapes in regal hues — purple, yellow, red, orange, blue, and gold — suspended from towering 20-foot ceilings. The way they sway in the gentle breeze feels like walking through the train of His Glory.

Can you feel that?

Surveying the room, I notice shadowed faces.
Some wear masks; others reveal anxious anticipation.
Yet, something is missing.
No one seems to be truly enjoying themselves.
The guests stand stiff and solemn, despite the music's inviting rhythm.
The melody calls for a soulful movement, but their hearts remain locked.

Then, there's the food — a feast fit for the finest of palates, enticing and rich.
Close your eyes and imagine the most exquisite dish you've ever tasted.

YASSS. It's that good.

Suddenly, a shift.
The energy changes.

From the top of a grand spiral staircase, the hostess finally emerges.
Conversations cease. Heads turn. Time itself seems to pause.

And then — without warning — a sound erupts into the atmosphere, cutting through the stillness.

Laughter

A deep, boisterous, infectious, unapologetic laugh rings out, shattering the solemn air like a thunderclap.
It reverberates through the house, sweeping through every room, filling every empty space.

The guests are stunned, caught off-guard. They don't yet realize what's happening.

She descends the stairs, her laughter rolling ahead of her like a mighty wave.
As she moves through the crowd, men drop to their knees, overcome by joy.
Women clap their hands, welcoming her presence.
The invisible has become visible.

Laughter — once hidden, thought of as something fleeting, something reserved for the young — is now here, standing in all her glory.
No longer tucked away. No longer underestimated.
The world will see her, experience her, and be transformed by what she has to offer.

It's not the sway of her hips that captures their attention, nor the confidence that radiates from her every step.
It's the joy.
The unmistakable, uncontainable joy written across her face, overflowing from her spirit.

Look at them now.
They're laughing.
Rolling on the floor, undone by the weight of joy.

Now the world can see what has always been inside of me.
My mystery is revealed.

From this day forward, I embrace the fullness of who I am.
No more running.

Every time I walk into a room, laughter is released.
Joy is experienced.
Gladness fills the atmosphere.
Laughter saturates every corner, leaving no space untouched.

You have now entered the presence of laughter.
And where laughter resides, healing follows.
Pain cannot stand in its presence.
Laughter and depression cannot occupy the same space — depression must leave.

My laughter is therapy.
It is a healing ointment, a balm for the soul.

"A joy-filled heart is curative balm, but a broken spirit hurts all the way to the bones."
(Proverbs 17:22, Voice)

My identity is rooted in the heart of God.
This is my purpose.
This is my calling.

I was created to fulfill God's desire on the earth — laughing all the way to the ends of the world and back.

God is Alpha and Omega, the Beginning and the End, the First and the Last.
God is Love.
God is Laughter.

"I am who I am by the grace of God."
(1 Corinthians 15:10, The Passion Translation)

I am God's laughter, released to turn the world back to the heart of the Father.
I have been sanctified, empowered, and set apart to prosper in every area of my life.

I have been blessed to laugh.

As you read this book, I declare that the Holy Spirit will release His power for laughter and joy through every written word.

I decree and declare:
When we laugh, the walls of grief, despair, abandonment, rejection, fear, and disease will crumble in the name of Jesus.

Laughter is here.
And nothing will be the same again.

Just like Sarah, God has graced me, Nandi Louise, with the gift of laughter!
Everyone who hears my story will laugh with me.

(Genesis 21:6, Voice)

Let's enter in.

Turn the page, the journey begins...

Chapter 1:
The Power Behind My Laughter

> "We are like common clay jars that carry this glorious treasure within, so that this immeasurable POWER will be seen as God's, not ours"
>
> — 2 Corinthians 4:7 (The Passion Translation).

Laughter saved me. In the darkest moments of my life, when grief threatened to drown me, it was laughter that pulled me back to the surface. But this wasn't just any laughter - it was laughter rooted in love, a divine gift that transformed my pain into strength. It took me years to understand this truth, but now I see it clearly: the power behind my laughter is love.

Being a caretaker for an elderly parent with deteriorating health is one of the most stressful experiences a person can endure. It's a role that demands strength, patience, and resilience, even when your own emotions feel like a storm-tossed sea. My mother was my world. She had battled lung cancer, dementia, and multiple strokes - each time defying the odds and leaving doctors in awe. She was a living miracle, and I was her anchor, her tower of strength. But inside, I was crumbling.

I'll never forget the day the nurse said those words. "There's nothing else we can do for your mom. She has six months to live. We're sending her back to the nursing home with hospice care."

It felt like a tidal wave crashing over me, sweeping away any evidence of control. All I could hear was the sound of water hitting the sand at a beach — WHOOSH! There goes all my emotions that were riding the surface of ocean waves safely, now scattered debris on the seashore. I don't even remember walking to my car. All I remember is sitting in the driver's seat, tears streaming down my face like an avalanche, destroying anything in its path, wondering how I would survive this.

Even in that moment of despair, I felt a flicker of hope. It was January, and my church was in the middle of our annual fast. That night, I dragged myself to Bible study, my heart heavy but my spirit searching. The guest speaker spoke about faith, and as I listened, something extraordinary happened. I had a vision — I saw my mother, healthy and whole, literally walking out of the hospital. It was so vivid, so real, that I clung to it with everything in me. From that day forward, I began confessing her healing, believing with every fiber of my being that she would walk out of that nursing home completely restored.

Six months passed, and my mother was still with us. But her spirit was restless. One Saturday, as I was getting ready to visit her, I received two phone calls. The first was from the nursing home psychologist.

"Your mother asked me something today," he said, his tone hesitant. "She wants to know why she's still here. Why hasn't God taken her yet?"

I paused, caught off guard. "What did you tell her?" I asked.

"I'm not sure what to say," he admitted. "What do you think I should do?"

I couldn't help but laugh. "Do something 'psychologie,'" I thought (though I knew that wasn't a word). Out loud, I said, "I don't know. You're the psychologist. You tell me."

Before I could process that conversation, immediately the hospice nurse called. "Your mother asked me why is she still here and why God hasn't taken her yet."

I sighed, bracing myself for another round of foolishness. But then the nurse added, "I told her, 'Maybe God needs time to prepare Himself, because you're a lot to handle.'"

I burst out laughing. It was the kind of laughter that comes from deep within, the kind that surprises you when you least expect it. The nurse started laughing too, and for a moment, the weight of everything lifted. "That's exactly what I was thinking, she is a hot mess!" I said, still chuckling.

In that moment, I realized something — even in the midst of pain, laughter could still find its way to the surface. It was a reminder that joy and sorrow couldn't coexist, and that love — even in its most complicated forms — could spark moments of lightness.

When I arrived at the nursing home that afternoon, my mother greeted me with her usual feistiness. "Stop praying for me!" she yelled.

"Nope, I will not," I replied. "If you go, then you go, but my prayers will not cease."

She sucked her one front tooth (yes, just one) and turned back to the TV, but I could see the strength in her eyes.

I sat down beside her, watching her for a moment. Then I asked softly, "Mom, why do you think you're still here?"

She shrugged her shoulders, her expression softening as if she were searching for the right words. For a moment, she didn't say anything. Then she turned her head toward me, her eyes locking onto mine. "I'm still here because of you baby girl," she said.

Her voice was tender but exhausted, and in that moment, I knew she was right. I wasn't ready to let her go. She was my only family, my anchor, and I clung to her with everything in me.

Transition day came like an unwelcome guest. It was September 24, 2015, and my mother's breathing had become shallow. She was no longer responsive, but I held her hand and spoke to her anyway. "Mom, Mom, Mom. Woman, answer me!"

When she didn't respond, I did what I always did when I didn't know what to do. I prayed. I leaned close to her ear and began speaking in my heavenly language (tongues), and to my surprise, she rapidly squeezed my hand. I opened the Bible to Romans (I don't even know why) and began reading aloud, my voice trembling but determined. And then I prayed one final prayer: "Father, I don't know when my mother last rededicated her life to You, but I know she belongs to You. My only request is that You personally walk her to heaven."

Immediately, I became aware of the presence of God. The room was overshadowed by the tangible presence of the Holy Spirit, and a gentle breeze brushed across my cheek, wiping away my tears. I could hear my father God's loving voice begin to speak to me.

The brightest light I had ever seen enveloped me, and I felt God hold me in His arms. His voice was tender yet filled with authority as He said, *"Daughter, you have no idea how much I love you. The power of your laughter is strong. You thought that the power behind your laughter was the result of all the trials and tribulations you've gone through. But that was not the power behind your laughter. You thought it was the Holy Spirit — and though the Holy Spirit was guiding you, even that was not the power behind your laughter. The power behind your laughter is LOVE. Your mother loved you the only way she knew how."*

His words washed over me, and I was overwhelmed with love and peace. I turned to my mother, I put her limp hand in mine, and gently placed it on my face. Tears streamed down my cheeks like water from an open faucet. "You were the best mother ever," I whispered. "I love you so much."

In that instant, she took her last breath - a sigh of relief. A light rose from her physical body, and I saw Jesus take her hand. Together, they walked out of the hospital and started their journey together to heaven. I burst into tears, not because she was gone, but because God heard my prayer and answered it. He had personally come to walk her to heaven.

The vision I had nine months earlier had come to pass. As God promised, she had indeed walked out of that hospital — healed, whole, and hand-in-hand with her true love, Jesus.

The power behind my laughter became my source of strength and stability. But what exactly is power? Power is purpose – divine purpose. It is inner transformation shape by God's sovereignty. It's the ability to act, to produce an effect, to influence. It's power exists beyond our control, yet it flows through us to bring about change. And when laughter is under the influence of love, it becomes a powerful force — one that can act, produce, and affect transformation in our lives.

Laughter rooted in love has the ability to *act* — to do something in the face of adversity. It has the ability to *produce* — to bring about results that defy our circumstances. And it has the ability to *affect* — to create an impact that shifts our perspective and heals our hearts. Laughter saturated with love becomes more than a sound – it is a sacred release of the anointing to minister, to up lift, and transform. When we allow love to fuel our laughter, it becomes a tool that helps us stand strong in the midst of grief, a lifeline that pulls us back from the edge of despair.

But here's the key: this power isn't ours alone. It comes from a source greater than ourselves. It's a reminder that even in our weakest moments, we are not alone (2 Corinthians 12:9). God gives us time to grieve, but grief is meant to be a season of healing, not a permanent dwelling place. When we allow Him to be our source of strength and stability, we open ourselves to the possibility of joy far beyond our understanding.

That awareness — the revelation knowledge of love — allowed me to step into freedom and transformation. For so long, I had recited Psalm 30:5, like a parakeet, repeating the words without fully understanding their depth: *"Weeping may endure for a night, but joy comes in the morning."*

Then one day, I read it in The Message translation (MSG), and I almost fell out on the floor. Actually, I did. It says, "The nights of crying your eyes out give way to days of laughter!"

The King James Version makes it sound like there's just one night of crying, followed by a single morning of joy. But let's be real, I didn't cry for just one night. I cried my eyes out for *many* nights. How about you — how many nights have you cried your eyes out?

But here's the beautiful truth: the moment I gave everything to God and began my laughter therapy, *days* of laughter followed. Not just one morning of joy, but days and days of it. And that's the promise for you too. "GOD WILL LET YOU LAUGH AGAIN; you will raise the roof with shouts of joy" (Job 8:21 MSG).

What's behind your laughter?

My journey through grief taught me that laughter truly is a medicine. "A merry heart doeth good like a medicine" (King James Version). Proverbs 17:22 is more than some old proverb — it's God's health insurance policy. Solomon testified that a merry, joyful heart can be as beneficial as medicine. Medicine is described as the practice and procedures used for the prevention and treatment of diseases and abnormal conditions. When laughter is practiced, it can provide a sense of relief, well-being, and positive changes to improve health.

While my story may be unique, the pain of loss is universal. Perhaps you're walking through your own valley right now, wondering how you'll find joy again. God promises in Matthew 5:4, "blessed are those who mourn, for they shall be comforted" (New King James Version).

I want to share with you a practice that helped me rediscover laughter even in my darkest moments.

Laughter Exercise: Activating the Power of Laughter

Laughter is more than just a reaction - it's practice, a tool, and a source of strength. This exercise is designed to help you tap into the transformative power of laughter, even when joy feels out of reach. Let's begin.

Step 1: Set the Scene
- Find a quiet, comfortable space where you can stand without distractions.
- Take a moment to center yourself and focus on God.
- Remind yourself that laughter is a frequency of love, and a way to reconnect with your inner strength.

Step 2: Breathe Deeply
- Stand tall, feet shoulder-width apart and relax your shoulders.
- Take a deep breath in through your nose, filling your lungs completely. Hold it for a moment and then exhale slowly through your mouth.

Step 3: Laugh with Intention
- On your next deep breath in, hold it for a moment, and as you exhale, let out a laugh. It doesn't have to be forced or loud - just a genuine, light laugh.
- Repeat this several times, each time allowing your laughter to grow a little louder, a little freer.
- If you feel silly at first, that's okay! Lean into it. Laughter is meant to be joyful and uninhibited.

Step 4: Build Momentum
- Once you've started, keep going. Let the laughter flow naturally. There is no need to think of anything funny.
- If your laughter feels forced at first, don't worry. Even forced laughter can trigger real joy. Keep going until it feels authentic.
- Continue for at least 1-2 minutes, or until you feel your heart rate slow down and your mind begins to clear.

Step 5: Reflect and Release
- When you're ready, let the laughter subside. Take a few deep breaths and notice how you feel.
- Ask yourself:
    - How does my body feel? Lighter? (Perhaps stronger, or more relaxed?)
    - How does my mind feel? Clearer? (Perhaps calmer, or more focused?)
    - How does my spirit feel? Renewed? (Perhaps refreshed, or revived; maybe both?)

Step 6: Praise (My Favorite Step)
- Invite God to laugh with you. I can tell you personally, He loves invitations and really loves to laugh.
- This is a great time to offer to God a prayer of thanksgiving.
- Give your hurt and grief to God

Step 7: Prayer:

Father, I invite you into my time of grief and pray that your loving arms will surround me like a comforting hug. As I navigate these difficult emotions, I need your peace to support me. Yet even in the storm of my emotions, I will cling to Your truth.

Thank you for the gift of laughter, that even in my pain, I can experience moments of lightness that remind me of your presence. I know You are here, walking with me through my grief. I trust that You are healing the shattered places within me in ways I cannot yet see or comprehend. Plant seeds of joy in the soil of my sorrow, that in time, my tears may give way to days of laughter.

Renew my hope, restore my strength, and remind me that Your love never fails.

In Jesus' holy and precious name, I pray, Amen.

Chapter 2:
Laughter is a Calling

> "The way to find your calling is to look at the way you were created. Your gifts have not emerged by accident."
>
> – Timothy Keller

I woke up this morning unaware that God was about to unveil a treasure hidden deep within me; a gift I didn't know I carried. It was an ordinary day, or so I thought. I went to work, sat at my desk, and lost myself in the rhythm of tasks and deadlines. But God had other plans. Little did I know this day would mark the beginning of a journey to discover my calling — a calling wrapped in laughter, unspeakable joy, and the unshakable truth of who I was created to be.

I was at my desk, focused on my work, when my supervisor's voice broke through the quiet. "Nandi, can you come into my office, please?"

I grabbed my notepad, my mind racing with possibilities. "Was it about a project? Was I being rewarded for the good work I have been doing?" I walked into her office, unaware of what was about to unfold.

She leaned back in her chair, her tone casual, almost nonchalant. "You're just too happy," she said, as if commenting on the weather. "You're too loud, and you laugh too loud. It's a disruption to the office. You work around a bunch of introverts. You need to tone it down."

I stood there, stunned. Too happy? Too loud? How do you tone down happiness? Speechless, I managed to nod and walked out of her office, her words hanging in the air like a thick fog. Each syllable seemed to echo in my mind, slicing through me like a chilling whisper in a horror movie. "Tone it down." But how? Was there some kind of Standard Operation of Procedures?

The Kidnapping

As I walked back to my desk, her words echoed in my mind, louder than any deadline I had to meet. They wrapped around me like heavy chains. My thoughts spiraled; the office became blurred around me. The fluorescent lights above seemed to dim, and the walls of the office faded away. What happened next was not physical, but a vision of the spiritual reality behind my struggle; a glimpse into the unseen realm where my true battle was taking place.

Suddenly, I wasn't there anymore. I stood on a narrow pathway, swallowed by thick shadows. The air was dense, almost suffocating, and cold whispers slithered through the darkness. I couldn't see where I was going, but I knew — I was being led somewhere I didn't want to go. I tried to shake off this feeling, trying to head back toward the light. It was too late, before I could turn back, rough hands seized me from behind. I twisted and fought back but it was no use. They were stronger, I was dragged further into the darkness, my laughter ripped away from me. I was in the battleground within my own mind.

The Three Hoodlums

I was surrounded by three demons. Shame jumped right in my face, its tone judgmental and belittling. You're too loud! No one will ever accept your laughter. It even laughed at its own joke, "Your laughter is so annoying. It's like an unwanted alarm at 3 a.m.; no one wants to hear it." In that moment, I felt myself shrinking into self-reproach, my confidence draining away.

Fear didn't just grip me — it **paralyzed** me. It said nothing, but its eyes were cold and merciless, slicing through me like a blade. I could read its mind, the words crawling through my soul like venom: Your laughter makes me cringe. You agitate others with your stupid cheer and joy. They don't want it. They tolerate you. You will never bring joy into this world.

Depression was the worst of them because it demanded my life. When depression spoke, its sound was hopeless; its whisper slithered into my ears. "Why even try?" it said, leaning in so close I could feel its breath — cold and lifeless. "You'll never be enough. Just give up. End it all. What's the point of fighting when you'll always lose?"

I looked around, desperate for an escape, and that's when I saw her — my laughter, bound and gagged in the corner. Her eyes were wide with concern, but she was fighting to break loose, her muffled cries pleading with me not to give up. I wanted to help her, to free her, but I felt paralyzed, defenseless against the onslaught of disapproval. Then, in the oppressive darkness, a sound — faint, but there. It was my laughter – muffled and bound, but refusing to be silent.

Unwitting Agents for the Enemy

I woke from that harrowing nightmare, my mind weighed down by a crushing realization. The battlefield in my mind had left me shaken, but the real fight was far from over. As I reflected on the battle, I began to see how those closest to me — friends, family, even coworkers — had unknowingly become pawns in a game orchestrated by the enemy. Their words and actions, though perhaps well-meaning, were chipping away at my joy, my laughter, my very essence. I questioned my significance. It was as though my true purpose had been buried beneath layers of doubt and oppression, and every interaction felt like another shove into an isolated corner.

"Shush," they'd say. "Hush." The words echoed in my ears, over and over, until I retreated into a space of self-condemnation and remorse. "Why are you yelling?" they'd ask. "Use your inside voice!" or "I'm standing right here. Lower your voice."

Each admonition felt like a blow, another crack in the foundation of my self-worth. "It doesn't take all that," they'd say dismissively. "That's too much laughter; this is a place of business," they scolded.

"You're having too much fun; get back to work," they demanded.

"No one laughs like that," they'd assert, their words like daggers to my already wounded spirit. "I think you're just looking for attention," they'd add, their judgment piercing through the fragile layers of my composure.

With each remark, shame tightened its grip, squeezing until I felt smaller and smaller. I began to lower not just my voice, but also my laughter and ultimately, my entire emotional outlook, dimming the light inside me to make others comfortable. But deep down, I knew something wasn't right. Why was my joy so threatening? Why was my laughter so offensive?

These were just mere acts of persecution, in its essence, means to disrupt, displace, or divert. It is the sinister attempt to drive us away from our strength, our greatness, and above all, our connection with God. The adversary trembles at the sight of our potential and endeavors to expel us from the divine presence, inflicting harassment, torment, and intimidation to lead us astray. His ultimate aim is to obscure our understanding of our purpose, to hinder us from fulfilling God's intentions for us on this earth. To erase our calling!

It took me a while to realize that the fight wasn't with the people around me. The Bible says, "We wrestle not against flesh and blood, but against principalities, against powers, against the rulers of the darkness of this world, against spiritual wickedness in high places" (Ephesians 6:12, KJV).

It's crucial to recognize that our battle isn't against mere mortal beings. My supervisor, for instance, was merely a pawn in the enemy's game, manipulated to sow seeds of doubt and discouragement in my path to discovering my calling. Let us not be deceived or diverted from the very reason for our existence.

The enemy - our adversary - is a tyrant, a mean oppressor. He's cruel. He'll use anyone and anything to make you retreat, to make you doubt yourself, to make you forget who you are. Why? Because he hates God and you. He sees the treasure inside you - the laughter, the joy, the light — and he knows that if you walk in your destiny, you'll destroy his plans for chaos. He'll do anything to disrupt God's plan for your life, even though deep down, he knows it's impossible. God's plans cannot be thwarted.

Too Loud for the Room

I remember being out to dinner with a good friend. She said something that was really funny, and I exploded with laughter. I must admit, even I heard the boom of my own voice. After all, Merriam-Webster defines laughter as an *explosive* vocal sound. Yup, it was definitely explosive — like an echo bouncing through an empty building.

As I caught my breath, I noticed my friend shifting uncomfortably. She glanced around the restaurant, her expression tight. "Shush, this is not the establishment for all that," she said.

I froze.

Her tone wasn't playful - she was embarrassed. I could see her humiliation, and immediately, I shrank. "Had I done something wrong?" I thought. I apologized, suddenly hyperaware of my own voice. For the rest of the night, I covered my mouth every time I laughed, as if it were something to be ashamed of. It was an unspoken chastisement — a punishment for an offense I hadn't even realized I committed. And just like that, I became a prisoner to melancholy.

I Was Born Loud

That night at dinner, I realized something — I had spent my whole life being LOUD. Not just in laughter, but in spirit. I didn't know how to shrink myself, and honestly, I didn't want to. But somehow, my joy was always an offense to someone. And that truth followed me everywhere, even into the workplace

For as long as I can remember, one word has defined me — LOUD. My personality exudes it. My voice carries it. Even my words on a page refuse to whisper.

I'm ENTHUSIASTIC and **bold.** It's not even by choice; it's simply the way I was conceived in the heart of God, with a larger-than-life personality that refuses to be contained. People have always told me to tone it down, shrink my voice, dial back my enthusiasm. Fit into their carefully measured expectations. But I never asked for the spotlight; it just found me — it gravitates toward me like a magnet drawn to its polar opposite. And even if I wanted to fade into the background, I wouldn't know how. Because this is who I am, authentically.

My laughter doesn't tiptoe into a room — it bursts through the doors, unashamed and alive. It's not just noise; it's

medicine, a force that carries healing in its wings (Malachi 4:2; New Living Translation). Yet, somehow, something so life-giving became an offense; a disruption; an irritation to those who don't understand its power.

I didn't fully understand how anyone could be uneasy around a joyful noise.

Like a joyous symphony, it carries the vibrancy of my spirit, unapologetically bold and uncontainable. It's a testament to the exuberance that defines me, a natural expression of the boundless enthusiasm that flows through my layers. Although I try to quiet it, my laughter refuses to be subdued, a constant reminder of the irrepressible force of my joy (1 Peter 1:8).

Isn't it strange that something as pure as laughter, meant to uplift; can be seen as a disturbance? That joy, the very thing we're wired to seek, somehow unsettles those who've forgotten how to embrace it. Yet, somehow it managed to disrupt the equilibrium of lives and workplaces. For me, bringing laughter and happiness to others is more than just a pastime – it is a source of fulfillment, a way of brightening someone else's day and momentarily escape my own struggles. Little did I realize that my laughter held the power to shift the emotional landscape of my environment, to uplift spirits and foster a sense of solidarity.

Beneath the mask of joy, beneath the lightheartedness that others saw, storms raged within me. Pain, deep-seated and oppressive, lay buried under years of verbal abuse and silent suffering. I wanted laughter to be my armor, a shield against the relentless persecution, but it had not yet become my refuge. Instead, it felt like a fragile defense, one that could shatter at any moment under the weight of others' judgments. I never imagined that my laughter, the very thing I longed to protect me, would eventually become a thorn in my side.

Compliance or Crisis?

After that first meeting with my supervisor, I became more cautious. I laughed less. I was quieter. I could feel myself shrinking, what choice did I have? Apparently, even my silence was being noticed. And then, to my surprise, two weeks later it happened again. I heard those familiar words. "Nandi, can you come into my office, please?"

I felt my stomach tighten. Not again. I walked into her office, bracing myself. "What now? Another complaint? Another warning to 'tone it down?'" I thought.

She exhaled, tilting her head slightly. "Are you okay?"

I blinked. "I don't understand your question," I said, my voice slow and deliberate.

She hesitated before continuing, her tone suddenly softer. "I've received multiple complaints that you haven't been yourself lately. We just want to make sure… that you're not going to hurt yourself."

I felt like I had been struck by lightning. Two weeks ago, I was too happy. Now I was too quiet.

AND NOW – I want to HURT myself?

How did my joy become a red flag? And how did my silence become a crisis? The irony of it all was just rude. I wanted to explain, to say something but the words wouldn't come. Instead, I just stood up and walked out, leaving her unfinished sentence hanging in the air.

I sat at my desk, stunned, replaying the conversation over and over in my head.

If I laughed, it was a problem.

If I was quiet, it was a problem.

What did they want from me?

I had spent so much time suppressing my joy that even my absence of laughter became suspicious. The world was watching, waiting to decide what version of me was acceptable. And I realized then I would never win their approval.

Laughter is a Calling

Nothing catches God by surprise. That same evening, I was home sitting in my office. I was numb, hollow. My chest was tight, my mind racing. The weight of rejection pressed against me like an iron hand.

And then, "Daaadddyyy!" The cry ripped from my throat before I could stop it.

I fell to my knees, sobbing uncontrollably. "Why?!" I exclaimed.

My words broke apart, choked by grief. I wanted to pray, but the pain was too thick, too heavy. All I could do was whisper, "Help me." "I want to keep my job. Then I begged My Father God, help me conform to what man wants. Help me to blend in and not cause a disturbance. I don't know what to do. I need you."

A sudden gust of wind rushed through my home, sending shivers down my spine. I gasped for air, my heart pounding, I fell flat on my face. Then, I heard His voice: *"Nandi, fear not. I am your Lord God, Almighty."*

And suddenly, I felt Him.

The Holy Spirit. His presence was deep, overwhelming, consuming like a soft, warm blanket all-encompassing me. He hugged me, pulled me in, surrounded me. I inhaled sharply, my body melting into His arms. Peace settled over me, steadying my soul. My weeping slowed, my entire being relaxed, the weight of my supervisor's words fading into insignificance. I needed to be comforted, so I gave in to His presence completely. My Daddy was here to see about His little girl.

God begins to speak. *"Here me when I say: You are fearfully and wonderfully made and created in MY image. I put my spirit in you. I gave you your personality and you are not to change it. It is not your personality to change. I have called you; set you apart for my purpose. I am sharing you as a gift of laughter to the world. Your laughter will cause healing; drive out depression and all manner of disease. Your smile will delight the hearts of men. For I have spoken, says the Lord. Know that I am with you always. From this day forward I call you 'Laughter to the Nations,'"* said the Lord. "Be courageous and strong."

There is something about the voice of a loving Father. His voice is comforting, soothing, like the sound of a wave rushing to the shore, like the warmth of a crackling fire, something reassuring. We were so close; I could feel the passion of His breath as He spoke.

"I am passionately in love with God because He listens to me. He hears my prayers and answers them. As long as I live, I'll keep praying to Him, for He stoops down to listen to my heart's cry" (Psalm 116:1-2, TPT).

I want to encourage you, God hears you. He listens to your prayers. He is concerned about what is happening in your life and personally checks in on you. God is not afar off; He is with you.

God called me "Laughter to the Nations." Your Father has called you also. When the world stood against me, Jehovah Gibbor came to fight for me. He is my ultimate heavyweight champion. What the world saw as annoying, God saw as my greatest strength. He turned my persecution into a passion and calling.

Do you Hear?

Whatever persecution you have endured, God turns it into your calling.

God engineered everything about you, your personality, your demeanor, your voice, your smile, your laugh. Nothing about you is accidental. Every single part of who you are was designed with purpose. God is very intentional.

"The call of God is not just for a select few but for everyone. Whether I hear God's call or not depends on the condition of my ears." — Oswald Chambers
What is the condition of your hearing? Are you listening to His call?

I want to challenge you to open your heart and allow yourself to hear God calling you to a specific purpose. Someone is waiting for you to step into your calling so they can be transformed. You are not here by accident. You carry the solution to someone's problem. You have a kingdom assignment.

Breaking Free from the Lies

The devil is the father of lies, but you don't have to live under his deception. It's time to break every agreement with his lies and step into God's truth and freedom. I had to overcome things that held me back, the

> "The call of God is not just for a select few but for everyone. Whether I hear God's call or not depends on the condition of my ears."
> — Oswald Chambers

pain that kept me silent. I had been buried alive, living like a zombie — moving, but lifeless.

My mother, in her own pain, spoke words that cut deep, words that told me I wasn't good enough. *"You're just like your father. You'll never be anything."* Every time she said those words, it was like a paper cut, tiny, but painful. Left untreated, those small cuts became infected wounds that threatened to destroy me. But God wanted me healed. I renounce the lies told to me that I was not enough. I accept God's truth over my life. I searched God's word and found myself.

Freedom wouldn't come easy, but it was possible.

It's time for you to break the agreement with the enemy. The agreement that you are not good enough or that you don't have a gift good enough to be used by God. I declare that every lie the enemy has told you is abolished and destroyed in the name of Jesus. I decree that you will walk in God's calling for your life. Just as I found freedom, it's time for you to break the agreement and realize your own freedom.

My Calling Against Darkness

Now, I know who I am. "Laughter to the Nations." This is no small thing. The enemy thrives in chaos, depression, and deception — building strongholds of heaviness that trap people in darkness. But laughter? Laughter is a spiritual weapon. It shatters the chains of anxiety, breaks the spell of despair, and punctures the illusion of hopelessness. When genuine laughter erupts, darkness simply cannot maintain its grip.

This is how I know — people call me on purpose just to laugh. One friend even calls me her personal jester. That is just too funny. Excuse me! I am not a clown. Well, maybe, just a little. These aren't just casual interactions. Friends will call me when their day is rough, when the weight feels unbearable, and before the conversation ends, we've gone from being stressed to chuckling to uncontrollable joy.

I hear their transformation through the phone: sighs of relief replacing tension, the sound of their voice filling with energy, the heaviness in their tone dissolves with each burst of laughter. I can literally hear the shift as their words begin to flow more freely, more hopefully. By the end of our call, they sound like different people — lighter, stronger, and restored — not just momentarily cheered-up, but spiritually unburdened.

Co-workers pour into my office, seeking relief from the weight of the day. When laughter fills the room, their burdens physically lighten, their minds clear of frustration, and creativity flows effortlessly. Research has proven that laughter can lead to creativity. Who knew? God. What the enemy meant for overwhelming pressure becomes an opportunity for breakthrough. This isn't just entertainment, it's liberation. Each laugh pushes back against the darkness trying to suffocate joy.

Laughter is not just a reaction, it's a calling. Now I understand why the enemy fought so hard to silence me. He understands the power of laughter and that it is intended to destroy all his works. My laughter has put me on the enemy's hit list. It fuels me – I laugh even louder.

God's Plan for You

Jeremiah 29:11 (Amplified Bible) reads as, "For I know the thoughts and plans that I have for you, says the Lord, thoughts and plans for welfare and peace and not for evil, to give you hope in your final outcome."

Thank You, Daddy.

Now, for the reader of this book, laugh! Right now. Just for a minute. Celebrate who you are and the victory that's already yours.

God knows exactly what He's doing — He's smart like that. After all, He is omniscient, the one who holds total knowledge of everything. Nothing catches Him off guard. Nothing surprises Him, and I know this as fact — lives depend on my obedience.

You have a divine assignment. When God calls, you don't have to fully understand why. You just need to believe and obey. He has given each of us countless opportunities to trust Him. And honestly? I've failed many of those tests. But here's the beautiful thing — He never stops calling.

I get it. We all have our own plans. I sure did. Before I even considered saying "yes" to God, I had my own agenda, my own timeline. I convinced myself that I needed to get my life together first before I could fully follow Jesus. But guess what? That was never His requirement. He wasn't waiting for me to be perfect — He was waiting for me to surrender.

Proverbs 3:5-6 tells us to trust in the Lord with all your heart and lean not on your own understanding.

That is exactly what we do, lean to our own understanding. Your understanding may fail you. Your own opinions can mislead you. But God does not change His mind when He calls someone. Romans 11:29 confirms that God's gifts and His call are irrevocable. Trust God and be humble enough to lean into His wisdom.

Your Decision: Will You Be Courageous Enough to Laugh?

I acknowledge that I am divinely appointed to laugh for the Kingdom of God. And everything in life starts with a decision. We decide what to eat, what to wear, what career to pursue, who to marry. But the most important decision is, will you walk in your calling? Will you embrace it, sharpen it in faith, and release it for impact?

I decided that nothing in my past would dictate my present or my future. I decided to be courageous enough to laugh.

Will you be courageous enough to trust God and step into your calling?

Prayer to Embrace Your Divine Assignment

Heavenly Father,

Thank you for your loving kindness and your tender mercies. You are the author of my life, the one who formed me with purpose before I ever took my first breath. You said if I need wisdom to ask and You would give it freely. I come before You with an open heart, asking for wisdom — I know you have placed a calling within me.

What have You called me to do? Reveal the gifts and callings You've placed within me and show me how to use them for Your glory. You have a tailor-made calling for me to reach other people. I desire to help others, make a difference, and transform lives. Show me what I am passionate about.

Teach me to trust Your plan, even when I don't understand it. Give me the courage to walk boldly in my calling, the joy to embrace it fully, and the faith to know that You will equip me every step of the way.

If laughter is my assignment, let me laugh freely. If my voice is my tool, let me speak boldly. Whatever You have placed in me, I surrender it back to You.

Lead me, Lord. I am listening.

In Jesus' name, Amen.

Take a moment after this prayer to sit quietly with God.

As you listen, consider these questions:

1. What brings you great joy?

2. What gifts have others affirmed in you?

3. What needs do you notice in others that break your heart?

Write down whatever comes to your heart — even if it surprises you. The intersection of these answers often reveals glimpses of your calling.

Chapter 3:
Laughter is Healing

"Your mind cannot heal without laughter. Your soul cannot heal without joy."

— Catherine Rippenger Fenwick

Laughter is often referred to as the best medicine, and Proverbs 17:22 remind us, a cheerful heart is good like medicine. While this verse is widely known, it's one of many scriptures that highlight the divine power of joy to heal.

Laughter was never an afterthought — it has always been part of God's design for our wholeness. From the beginning, He placed laughter in our emotional makeup, a divine provision designed to heal, restore, uplift, and strengthen us; physically, mentally, and spiritually. Its power cannot be underestimated. Today, science is finally catching up to what scripture has long declared, recognizing laughter not only as a source of joy but as a powerful tool for medical and mental health.

You Don't Have to Be Funny

You don't have to be a comedian or a clown to use laughter for healing. The truth is something doesn't have to be funny for the effect of laughter to work. You just need to Laugh Out Loud on Purpose (LOLP).

In a world that can feel overwhelming and too serious, laughter offers a much-needed antidote. It provides an escape from stress, worry, and a host of other destructive challenges, offering a glimpse of relief and joy — even in the darkest of times.

The Light of God

I had finally woken up from a diabetic coma. You'd think after being in a coma for days, I'd wake up well-rested, right? Like a deep sleep... Think again. I was totally exhausted.

As I drifted in and out of consciousness, I noticed close friends hovering around me; some praying, some just ... being there. Then, one of my sista-friends showed up. It was the first time I'd been fully awake for hours, and she was so relieved to see me conscious. Naturally, she wasted no time filling me in on all the dramatic details of my brush with death.

Then, she got serious. She leaned in, eyes full of curiosity, and asked, "Gurl, tell me the truth... did you see the light?"

"Light?" I blinked, confused. "What light?"

"You know, God's light."

I looked around the room, checking to see who else was there. I wasn't about to say anything that would get me committed to a mental institution. I whispered, "Gurl, come here."

She leaned in closer, eyes sparkling like a diamond ring; a little too eager, like a detective on a case. "Did you see the light of God? Did you go to heaven? What does Jesus really look like?"

I checked the room again, her eyes locked on me, waiting for a big revelation. So, I looked her dead in the eye and, with all the drama I could muster, I whispered:

"I didn't see no damn light ... and I wasn't looking for it neither."

And just like that, I lost it!

I burst out laughing and couldn't stop. The laughter echoed off the walls, shaking my already weak body. I laughed so hard, I couldn't breathe. Don't judge me, I even cried a little — between my legs. Yeah, it was that funny.

She jumped back, her face shifting from confusion to surprise. And if looks could kill — well, you know the rest. But then, slowly, her expression softened. A smile crept onto her face. She sucked her teeth and muttered, "You are so silly. You get on my nerves."

Then, she hugged me, and she started laughing too.

The room filled with our laughter, almost like it was a friend walking in to check on us. It was healing. It was joy. It was exactly what I needed in that moment.

And that's when it hit me, laughter had been there for me all along. Through every trial, every heartbreak, every moment of despair, laughter refused to leave me. Even on the edge of death, she showed up, determined to remind me to live. Laughter is my friend.

It wasn't my time to go — not because I fear death (because I don't), but because I refuse to leave this earth without making an impact. Taking God's laughter to every corner of the world is my personal goal.

My purpose is clear: to help as many people as I can walk in the fullness of joy. My work in God's kingdom is just getting started. Sure enough, laughter — my laughter — is making her presence known.

Laughter is Healing

Healing is woven into the very fabric of God's character, and His power brings complete restoration. The World Health Organization defines health as a state of complete physical, mental, and social well-being — not just the absence of disease. But how much more does our Creator, the one who designed our very being, care about our healing?

God has His own divine healthcare plan and it is free.

He is Jehovah Rapha, "The Lord who heals you." In Hebrew, Rapha means to completely make whole, to thoroughly mend and repair, to restore health in full. God isn't just treating symptoms, He is committed to your complete wholeness in mind, body, and spirit.

When God first spoke the prophetic word into my life and changed my name to "Laughter to the Nations," I had no idea what it truly meant. Slowly, I began to see how laughter was not just a source of happiness, but a source of healing and wholeness.

Laughter Kairos Moment: Migraine Healed

One Saturday evening, I was enjoying dinner at a seafood restaurant with a friend. It was a normal evening or so I thought. Unaware, a divine encounter was about to unfold.

As we were preparing to leave, a woman approached me urgently. The look on her face stopped me in my tracks. Concern flashed across my mind, but curiosity took over. What was wrong? Why did she look at me like that?

She wasted no time, her words spilling out in a rush. She began pouring out her heart, sharing her battle with chronic migraine headaches. How loud noises irritate her. OMG! Was this another complaint about me being too loud? I thought to myself.

For context, chronic migraines aren't just bad headaches. They are completely disabling. Imagine head-splitting pain for 15 days or more a month, each episode lasting for hours, sometimes days. The kind of pain that leaves you unable to function, forcing you into isolation.

Migraines don't just bring pain, they bring light and sound sensitivity, nausea, vomiting, muscle weakness, and even insomnia. Stress makes them worse, and in many cases, nothing seems to help. It's suffering in a way that few people truly understand.

As she shared her struggles, something miraculous happened. Despite the noisy environment of the restaurant, she told me that my laughter was easing her pain. With every burst of laughter, her pain faded. Until suddenly... it was completely gone. She was overwhelmed with gratitude. By faith, she was confident that it was MY laughter, my joy, that had healed her.

At first, I didn't quite understand what she meant. Normally sound sensitivity is one of the most debilitating symptoms of migraine headaches. By all logic, my laughter should have irritated her pain, made it worse. Nothing is logical about God's healing power (1 Corinthians 1:27). So instead, laughter became a sound of healing. This was an expression of God's love and compassion for His people.

> By faith, she was confident that it was MY laughter, my joy, that had healed her.

As she spoke, I was overwhelmed by the magnitude of what was unfolding. I had been doubting whether I was truly walking in my calling, and here God was, showing me, in the most tangible way, that laughter was indeed His tool of healing in and through me. In that very moment, I felt the undeniable presence of God.

He whispered, *"Do you see now? Do you understand? I told you that your laughter would heal."*

This wasn't a coincidence. This wasn't by chance. This was God's promise, fulfilled before my very eyes. This was a Kairos moment, an appointed time where everything aligned according to God's perfect plan (Psalms 138:8).

Preparation for Greater Faith

As I meditated on that divine encounter at the restaurant, I realized God was building my confidence in my calling and a pattern of testimony in my life. Let's face it, I wasn't very confident, and I needed my dad (creator) to encourage my faith. What happened with the migraine was no isolated incident — it was the beginning of God revealing how He would use laughter as a tangible healing force through me.

This experience confirmed something deeper about my calling. While the migraine healing showed me how laughter could bring immediate physical relief, God was about to demonstrate that laughter's power could go even further — confronting life-threatening disease head-on.

When I think about it, I see how God was gradually increasing my faith, preparing me for bigger challenges and bolder acts of obedience. He was teaching me, moment by moment, that when laughter is yielded to Him in faith, there are no limits to its healing power. Little did I know that my next encounter would require even greater courage and stretch my faith in ways I never imagined.

Laughter and Faith: Breast Cancer Healed

One Sunday, after sharing my testimony about how God had used laughter as a tool to defeat the enemy, a woman approached me, her eyes filled with excitement.

"I've been looking for you!" she exclaimed, gratitude pouring from her voice. "I heard what you said about laughing at the devil, and I decided to do just that. I laughed at the enemy during my chemo."

She went on to share her battle with cancer and how everything changed when she chose to laugh.

"Something was different," she said. "Usually, after chemo, I'm sick to my stomach. I vomit, my skin turns black, and I'm exhausted. But last week, after chemo, I went home, cooked dinner, and sat down with my husband. He looked at me and asked if I'd had chemo that day because I looked different. I felt different."

It wasn't until she looked in the mirror that she realized that nothing had changed physically. Her skin, normally darkened by chemo, looked normal. She hadn't vomited. She felt amazing.

"Laughter and prayer worked!" she said, her voice trembling with awe.

A Divine Instruction

As she spoke, I felt the Lord nudging me.

"Ask her what type of cancer she has."

I obeyed. "What kind of cancer do you have?"

"Breast cancer," she replied.

Then, God gave me an instruction that shook me to my core.

"Put your mouth on her breast and laugh."

Wait... what?!

"Really, God?" I thought. "You know I don't want to be anywhere near some woman's breast, right? Ha!"

But even in my discomfort, I knew I had to obey.

"I'm going to pray for you," I said, choosing faith over logic, "and the Lord has instructed me to laugh at your breast."

Without hesitation, she lifted her hands toward heaven. Her willingness gave me courage. So, I began to laugh at her breast, commanding healing, declaring that all breast cancer must flee in Jesus' name. As I prayed, I could feel the Holy Spirit's power flowing through me.

Then, suddenly, she fell to the floor, completely overcome by the power of God. I continued to laugh over her entire body, from head to toe, declaring that disease had no hold on her.

I was reminded of Psalm 27:13 (The Message):

"Bad guys have it in for the good guys, obsessed with doing them in. But God isn't losing any sleep; to Him, they are a joke with no punchline."

Indeed, cancer was a joke without a punchline here. The enemy's plan to destroy this faith filled woman was not going to work.

The Miraculous Testimony Revealed

Months later, I attended a prophetic conference in Washington, DC. During a break, a woman rushed toward me, her enthusiasm unmistakable.

"It's you!" she exclaimed. "Do you remember me? I had breast cancer, and you prayed for me months ago!"

As I looked at her, her face came into focus, and I remembered.

"How are you?" I asked.

Her eyes sparkled with joy.

"I'm cancer-free!" she declared. "My doctor did a test, and they couldn't find any trace of cancer. Your laughter healed me!"

I was so overcome by the Holy Spirit that I fell to my knees, praising God for His faithfulness. I thought of Isaiah 58:8, "Then your light will break out like the dawn, and your healing (restoration, new life) will quickly spring forth" (AMP).

O Lord, our Healer, we cry out for a miracle — and You heal! We declare that Your glory will break through as the morning, and our health shall spring forth speedily. Your righteousness shall go before us, and the Glory of God will be our healing.

> "I'm cancer-free!" she declared. "My doctor did a test, and they couldn't find any trace of cancer. Your laughter healed me!"

The Power of Laughter — A Life-Changing Tool

The work God has started in me is real. Laughter, my laughter, isn't just about spreading cheer or positive psychology; it's about transformation. It's about healing. It's about making an impact.

As I surrender to God, I grow more confident in the purpose He has called me to. Through these powerful experiences, I've seen firsthand how laughter, when combined with faith, brings healing and restoration.

It doesn't matter where I am — a restaurant, a church, an airport, a hospital, at work, or on the streets — the healing power of laughter is always available.

I've met countless people who have shared how my laughter: brightened their darkest days, brought emotional healing, and even prevented suicide. Laugher is more than just a reaction to humor, it is a supernatural force, a healing gift from God that can change your life and the lives of those around you. So, I ask you:

Will you be courageous enough to laugh?

Will you trust God to use your laughter as a tool for healing, breakthrough, and transformation?

Because of faith - I was courageous enough to laugh.

Now, it's your turn.

Prayer: The Healing Power of Laughter

Heavenly Father,

I come before You with a heart full of gratitude and joy. You are Jehovah Rapha — the Lord Who Heals — and Your power brings complete restoration to our bodies, minds, and spirits.

Today, I speak to the spirit of infirmity and declare that sickness, disease, and pain must flee! I command depression, anxiety, and every mental stronghold to loosen its grip in the name of Jesus. The joy of the Lord is our strength, and laughter — Your divine medicine — flows through us, bringing healing and breakthrough.

Lord, You sit in the heavens and laugh at the plans of the enemy (Psalm 2:4), and today, we choose to join You in that laughter. We laugh at sickness. HaHa! We laugh at fear. HaHa! We laugh at every lie the enemy has tried to speak over our lives, because we know the truth, You have already won the victory!

Father, I pray for every person reading this. Fill their hearts with uncontrollable, unstoppable, healing laughter. Let joy bubble up from within them, even in the midst of trials. May their laughter be a weapon against darkness, a balm for the brokenhearted, and a declaration of faith in Your goodness.

Lord, let them experience what I have experienced, the miraculous power of laughter in the face of the impossible. May their joy be contagious, their laughter a testimony, and their faith unwavering.

I declare that healing is springing forth like the morning light (Isaiah 58:8). Bodies are being restored. Minds are being renewed. Spirits are being lifted. And from this day forward, laughter will no longer be just a reaction, but a revelation, a sign that You are working, You are moving, and You are healing.

In Jesus' name, we receive it, we rejoice in it, and we laugh in victory.

Amen and HA-llelujah!

Chapter 4:
Laughter is a Gift

Your talent is God's gift to you. What you do with it is your gift back to God."

— Leo Buscaglia

He was the most desired man in the room. The crowd pressed in, everyone seeking His attention. But, when He saw her, His eyes locked onto her, steadfast, as if no one else in the room existed. She was radiant, more captivating than anyone He had ever seen. He saw her fully, like the one who formed her in the secret place.

His heart stirred, longing for her to notice Him. With the grace of a lion, He moved through the crowd, confident, each step deliberate, unstoppable. Yet, she remained unaware of His pursuit, until the moment she turned her head. Without warning, they were face to face.

He opened His mouth to speak. "Hello, sweetie," He said. His voice was smooth and magnetizing. She gasped softly.

"You don't remember when we first met when you were a little girl?" Jesus asked.

She blinked in shock. "Jesus?"

He chuckled, looking at her with unshakable affection. "You never cease to make Me laugh."

Embarrassment washed over her, and she looked down, avoiding His gaze. "No," she whispered.

Jesus smiled. "We used to play together in heaven. You would sit on My lap, laughing. We laughed all the time. We had so much fun. Those were good times."

"I would throw you high into the air, catching you in My arms, and you trusted Me completely. You never had any fear of falling." He sighed, "I miss those days."

Her heart pounded as He continued.

"You would laugh so hard that your laughter turned into drops of oil, filling heaven with delight. I knew that when I sent you to earth, I would breathe that very gift inside of you to impact the world with your laughter."

Tears welled up in her eyes.

Jesus took a step closer, His presence overwhelming.

"You are loved. You are treasured. And now, I am going to rush through your innermost being like a tsunami with My laughter. Now go. Go and fill the innermost being of others with laughter. And know this — I am always with you. Be strong and courageous."

Heaven Sent You

Wow. Can you even imagine?

This wasn't just a dream, it was an open vision I had during a Sunday church service, deep in worship. In a room full of worshipers, Jesus passed by every other soul and came straight to me.

Why?

To reveal a truth I had never fully grasped — that my laughter was a divine gift, one I had been using long before I ever took my first breath. I saw myself in heaven, playing with the Father, laughing in His presence. And He knew, even then, what He was going to do. He would ensure that laughter and joy would flood His creation, breaking the grip of darkness.

Pause and think about that.

You, too, once lived in heaven with your Father before He sent you here carrying a gift, a unique talent, skill, ability, or anointing that the world needs. Your gift carries the power of heaven, God, has entrusted you with a supernatural gift, meant for His glory. You literally were born with your Kingdom assignment.

What is a Gift?

A gift is something freely given, without expectation, without cost, and without condition.

- The Gift of God is a power or ability, bestowed naturally or supernaturally, for the purpose of serving Him. (*SimplyBible.com*)
- A gift is something given without expecting payment or anything in return. (*Wikipedia.com*)
- A gift is a natural ability or talent, willingly placed in someone's hands. (*Oxford Dictionary*)

God's gifts are all of these and more.

Before you were even formed, living in heaven, God placed a divine gift inside of you, one that carries His power, His anointing, and His purpose. This gift was never meant to be hidden or ignored. It was meant to be used. Laughter is a gift. Healing is a gift. Creativity is a gift. Encouragement is a gift.

Every ability, every talent, every anointing flows from the hands of God, and He freely gives these gifts — not because we've earned them, but because of His grace, His love, and His divine purpose for our lives.

And here's the most beautiful part: You already have your gift. You don't have to chase it, earn it, or prove yourself worthy of it. It's already dwelling within you, waiting to be used for His glory.

The only question is... will you use it?

God Knows You

Eternal One: Before I even formed you in your mother's womb, I knew all about you. Before you drew your first breath, I had already chosen you to be My prophet to speak My word to the nations (Jeremiah 1:5, Voice).

God knows you personally and has already chosen you. Before you took your first breath, He had already planned your purpose. So what if you're quirky? Different? Not like everyone else? That's exactly how God intended it.

I once heard someone say, "Be yourself: because everyone else is already taken."

And they were right. God didn't create copies — He created originals. He handcrafted you with a unique purpose, a distinct personality, and a gift that no one else can carry quite like you.

Just embrace it.

Because the world doesn't need another version of someone else.

We need you.

Disqualified?

And yet, we still search for validation outside of ourselves. Searching for validation from others. We let insecurities convince us that we are unworthy, unqualified, or not significant enough to carry out God's calling. We measure ourselves through the eyes of others, allowing their opinions to determine whether we are fit to walk in the gift God gave us. Therefore, we convince ourselves that we don't have a gift. That we're not special enough.

But let me ask you something — who told you that?

It wasn't God.

God hand-selected you for His purpose. He is not some corporate CEO that lets you get lost in the masses. He knows every single intricate detail of your existence, and He called you. He knows all the mistakes, all the lies, the life you are living and yet, He still called you.

"Thanks be to God for His indescribable gift!" (2 Corinthians 9:15, New King James)

And here's the funny part — for years, I struggled with even accepting the gift of laughter. I didn't see it as a gift at all. I wanted to sing. I wanted to play an instrument. I wanted something that felt "worthy" of being a gift.

Laughter? That wasn't a gift. That was just me being me (or so I thought). But, God doesn't make mistakes. He doesn't hand out gifts at random. He places purpose inside of us with intention. And when I finally stopped fighting it — when I embraced what He had already placed inside of me — that's when I discovered the truth:

Your gift isn't just about what you want. It's about what God wants to do through you.

God Qualifies You

I remember a time when I was asked to speak at a professional organization — and I turned them down. I didn't think I had the credentials to do it. The agenda was full of psychologists, nurses, therapists, professionals who had been using laughter therapy for years. I didn't see myself as one of them. What did I have to offer?

Later that day, while praying about something completely unrelated, God interrupted me with one simple question:

"Why do you disqualify yourself for something I have already qualified you for?"

I was ashamed. I had completely ruled out that my laughter, my joy, was the power of God. His gift to the world. That moment changed me. I realized that every gift God gives is good and perfect (James 1:17). The Bible tells us that your gifts will make room for you and bring you before great men (Proverbs 18:16). When you embrace the gift, be obedient to God, doors of opportunity will open.

You were born with a unique gift and a divine purpose. You don't have to search for it in the world around you — God already freely gave it to you.

Before you ever took your first breath, you were in heaven, waiting. Waiting for that divine moment when God would breathe a tailor-made gift into your very being, a gift designed not just for you, but for your church, your community, your workplace, your family.

Your gift is a solution to the world's problem.

Selah.

Pause. Let that sink in.

Meditation Exercise: Discovering Your Heavenly Gift for Your Earthly Purpose

You were not an accident.

Before you ever took your first breath, God knew you. He formed you with intention, purpose, and a divine gift meant to impact the world.

Don't rush through this. It's time to practice spending time in God's presence. If you want to, find Christian/Gospel instrumental music to play (I like "Rick Pino").

But now, it's time for you to see it for yourself.

- Find a quiet place: Begin by settling into a quiet and relaxed space where you can be undisturbed.

- Close your eyes: Allow your eyes to gently close.

- Take several deep breaths: Inhale deeply and exhale slowly, centering yourself.

- Imagine yourself in heaven with God: Visualize yourself in the divine presence of God. The atmosphere is filled with peace, joy, and radiant light.

- Walk around for a while: Explore this heavenly realm. What do you see? What do you hear? Take in the details and sensations around you.

- Spend time with God: See yourself engaging with God, sharing moments and conversations with Him.

- Seek revelation: Let the Holy Spirit reveal to you the purpose and gifts you were doing before you were sent to earth.

- Write down your experience: Capture what you see and hear in writing. Note any insights or revelations you receive.

- Trust God's guidance: Whatever you observed, trust that God has placed this unique gift within you to share with the world.

- Embrace your gift: Now, will you embrace this gift and walk in the path He has set for you?

- Reflect and meditate: Daily I will worship you passionately and with all my heart. My arms will wave to you like banners of praise. I overflow with praise when I come before you, for the anointing of your presence satisfies me like nothing else (Psalms 63: 4-5, TPT)

Chapter 5:
Laughter is a Weapon

Laughter is a powerful weapon that carries light. To laugh is to defy the darkness.

— Isobelle Carmody

Mark Twain, the legendary American humorist, once said, "The human race has one really effective weapon, and that is laughter." He understood what many of us are only beginning to grasp: laughter is more than entertainment — it's a transformative force, a weapon against darkness, and a divine instrument for spiritual warfare.

Twain saw laughter as a tool for coping with life's challenges, but God has shown me it's even more than that. It's spiritual warfare – it's not just some church concept either. The devil is trying to take you down – affecting your emotions, your relationships, and how you respond when life throws some shade your way.

In the ongoing battle between good and evil, laughter is a weapon — a divine instrument to dismantle the enemy's schemes and strengthen our faith. A weapon, by definition, is something used to defend, defeat, or gain an advantage. In the spiritual realm, laughter is exactly that — a weapon designed to overthrow the enemy and fortify our faith.

> In the spiritual realm, laughter is exactly that — a weapon designed to overthrow the enemy and fortify our faith.

God will not leave you unarmed. Just like you wouldn't bring a knife to a gunfight, God gives you specific weapons — one of these is laughter. Bring it to the fight.

Paul tells us that our battles are not against flesh and blood but against spiritual forces of evil (Ephesians 6:12, New

International Version). To fight these battles, God has given us spiritual weapons. In 2 Corinthians 10:3-4, Paul also writes, "For although we live in the natural realm, we don't wage war with human weapons or manipulation. Instead, our spiritual weapons are energized with divine power to effectively dismantle the enemy's defenses" (TPT). These weapons include prayer, faith, the Word of God, and — as I've discovered — laughter.

Our Personal Bodyguard

Laughter became my defense mechanism in times of spiritual attack. In a dream, God revealed Himself as Jehovah Gibbor, the Mighty Warrior (Psalm 24:8), and surrounded me with His presence like a shield. He instructed me to laugh and not stop. I began to laugh relentlessly. As I obeyed, my laughter became a shield all around me, deflecting the enemy's fiery darts and rendering them powerless. Those darts disintegrated into midair and blew away like dust.

Now look at our God — He's not just sitting up in heaven watching you struggle. When He reveals Himself as Jehovah Gibbor, that's God saying, "I'm your Mighty Warrior. I'm your Champion. I'm your Bodyguard. I'm the one who fights battles you can't even see."

This isn't some distant God who's too busy for your problems — this is the God who steps right into your situation, sword drawn, ready to defend you when you can't even lift your head to fight.

Ephesians 6:16-18 reminds us, "Be prepared. You're up against far more than you can handle on your own. Take all the help you can get, **every weapon God has issued**, so that when it's all over but the shouting, you'll still be on your feet" (Message Translation).

Laughter, rooted in faith, is one of those weapons. It's not just a reaction to humor but a deliberate act of spiritual warfare. You will learn to laugh intentionally, cause stress to scatter, resist temptations, and walk in peace. So be encouraged beloved, together, let's laugh boldly, laugh by faith, and watch as God turns our laughter into victory.

Weapon of Mass Destruction

The word of God reminds us to be vigilant because our adversary the devil, as a roaring lion, walks about seeking whom he may devour but we got something for him as soon as he turns that corner. We have four types of ammunition — (1) love, (2) joy, (3) forgiveness, and (4) praise loaded and ready to fire at the enemy's attacks.

When rejection tries to come for you, boom — counter with Love. If despair has you feeling like you're drowning, joy busts through like a life raft! When someone's words cut deep, and offense wants to take root, forgiveness pulls that mess by the roots before it can grow.

When everything feels like it's falling apart, praise shifts focus back to our Father who's never lost a battle. The enemy doesn't know what to do when you start fighting with these weapons.

Ammunition of Love

When love connects with laughter, we gain an advantage over the enemy to conquer anything. Unity is the result. Because love is so personal, it carries countless thoughts, ideas, and definitions. But true love is the opposite of man's understanding. 1 Corinthians 13 (Message translation) describes love this way: "So, no matter what I say, what I believe, or what I do, I'm bankrupt without love. Love never gives up. **Love cares more for others than self.** It isn't always "me" first; it doesn't fly off the handle, and **doesn't keep score of sins of others**. (That's true forgiveness). Puts up with anything. It never looks back." Take time to read the full chapter — it's life-changing.

Growing up, all my girlfriends seemed to have close, loving relationships with their mothers. I watched as they created happy memories that would last forever. I wasn't jealous but I wanted that. While I knew my mother loved me, our connection lacked the depth and closeness I longed for. It was as if we were on different pathways going in our own direction.

Now all grown up, all things are possible. With that longing still in my heart and a little more mature, I started praying for a better relationship with my mom.

Over several months, eager I poured my heart out to God. "I want a relationship with my mom."

Finally, when He answered, His response surprised me, *"Start attending the marriage ministry meetings at your church."*

"Now what?! God, I don't even have a husband," I thought. "Wait, you found me a man?!"

His laughter filled the atmosphere as He said, *"Silly girl, a relationship is a relationship, no matter the elements and roles."*

"Uhm, is that a 'no' on the husband front? What do You mean?" I asked, curiously yet a little confused.

"They all require the same elements to thrive — trust, respect, communication, and understanding," replied the Most High.

Desperate for a relationship with my mom, I decided to obey. There I was, the only single person in a room full of married couples. A few weeks later, I was asked to assist the instructors teaching "Marriage and Ministry" at the School of Ministry.

"Otay?! God, isn't this a bit much?" I thought, half-laughing, half-wondering what His plans were.

Instead of complaining (which I did often), I learned to communicate, to listen, to be supportive, and to understand my mom's perspective. And yes, I even learned how to forgive (ugh). Slowly, I began to apply these principles to my relationship with my mom. It wasn't easy, but it was necessary.

I remember during one of those marriage meetings, my pastor said something that completely shifted my perspective: "God uses marriage and spouses to express His love for you on earth. I'm in love with God first. If I were to fall out of love with my husband, it would mean I've fallen out of love with God. And I could never fall out of love with God."

Wow. That shifted my perspective. While I'm not "in love" with my mom in the romantic sense, I realized I am deeply in love with God. And through that love, God was showing me how to express His love for her. He was teaching me to see her through His eyes — not as the person who had hurt me, but as someone He loved unconditionally. Through God's lens, I began to see the power of His love working in our relationship. Ultimately, all I wanted was to love my mom unconditionally, no matter what. With God's help, I learned that love isn't just a feeling — it's a choice, a commitment, and a reflection of His heart.

Abandoned

To understand our relationship, you need to know our history. My mother abandoned me at four years old, leaving me with a childcare provider. My father, who was living above a bar at the time, wasn't in a position to care for me, so I stayed with this woman for a year. When I finally came to live with my mother, the wounds of rejection and abandonment ran deep — barriers that would take years to heal. Do I dare to say we were not close by any means?

The Journey of Forgiveness and Laughter

I wanted a real relationship with my mother.

Here comes the hard work. I sat down for what I like to call a "courageous conversation." Where truth meets vulnerability – head on.

"Mom, I want us to be close."

She smiled. "Oh, Babygirl, I want that too!"

"What do you need from me?" I asked.

"How about spending time with me? We could talk or watch a movie together."

Inside, I screamed, *"HELL NO!"* (Okay, yes, I cursed in my mind. I asked God for forgiveness about a month later.) Reluctantly, instead of giving in to those thoughts, I opened my mouth and spoke from my heart: "This will be hard … but yes."

Baby steps. That's how we built our relationship. It takes time and effort. I chose not to retreat to my room. I chose to sit with her. To talk. To laugh. And, to my surprise, I started enjoying it.

One day, she shared her deepest secret, that leaving me was the hardest thing she ever had to do. Then she disclosed the time she tried to take her own life and showed me those faint scars on her wrist. In that moment, an overwhelming compassion fell over me. How could I have never noticed her scars before?

I say this from the depths of my heart — STOP holding your parents hostage for their wrongdoings. They have suffered too. They have their own story. At some point, you have to stop blaming them for everything that went wrong in your life. Yes, they hurt you; I acknowledge that, but release them so you can walk in true freedom and restore your relationships. Someone has to be courageous enough to break the generational curses that plague our families.

The Power of Love and Laughter

We even went on a cruise together. I truly expected to hear "man overboard" at some point. However, God warned me on the second night, *"You are NOT allowed to push her overboard."*

"God, you take the fun out of everything," I giggled to myself.

In the end, love and laughter brought us together. When laughter connects with love, it becomes a weapon — an advantage over the enemy. It broke down barriers of anger, disappointment, and resentment. It made space for healing, for joy, and for unity.

> STOP holding your parents hostage for their wrongdoings. They have suffered too.

What will YOU do to break the barriers in your broken relationships? Have you ever considered that joy might be a tool for healing? Could laughter be the unexpected key to forgiveness?

It's time to set yourself free.

Ammunition of Joy

In the presence of God is the fullness of joy, complete satisfaction and total dependence on Him. When you follow God, joy overflows. But His presence isn't just about comfort; it's also where battle plans, strategic moves, and tactics are revealed. Gratitude is one of those tactics; it inspires joy. Joy is internal, a fruit of the Spirit that can be developed. It's one of God's greatest characteristics. When you allow joy to break out into laughter, you become completely developed and satisfied.

I have always had this unspeakable joy, and honestly, it is genuine. One of the meanings of my name, Nandi, is "to be joyous and satisfied." Hahahaha! Now that's funny. My very nature is joy. I'm not just filled with it — I *am* a source of it. When I laugh, joy spills into the atmosphere, releasing healing.

My laughter is so distinct that friends call me just to tap into my joy supply, often saying, 'I need to laugh.' Even at work, coworkers flock to my office, seeking a break from the daily drama and a dose of lighthearted relief.

Joy as a Weapon in the Workplace

Knowing who I am in God, I *had to* activate this unspeakable joy in the workplace. In reality, I was already operating in it, but I hadn't yet realized its power.

I had a supervisor who was downright mean. She spoke to me with disrespect, took credit for my ideas, and undermined me at every turn.

Side Bar: You do *not* have to tolerate disrespect from anyone. I have always had an innate ability to speak my mind directly and *professionally*. Let me say it again — professionally. I have always related to Peter in the Bible — a master with a sword. I'll cut off your ear and thank Jesus that He's nearby to put it back on. I have a mouth on me. Thank God my mouth is under His direction now. For years, I thought I needed to defend myself. But no — God defends me. It took time and many tests to learn that lesson.

Back to my story. I shared an office with this supervisor and another coworker. One day, my supervisor was in an unusually nasty mood, yelling at me for no reason. I kept a sincere smile on my face. "I'm sorry you're having a bad day," I blurted out. "I'm going to take a laughter break." Then I walked out.

It's okay to remove yourself from a situation before it escalates.

My other officemate followed me into the hallway. She said, "You are so full of laughter and joy." You really love God because you treat this woman with great respect — even though she's so mean to you. I *now* know that God is real."

That moment was significant because she didn't believe in God. Proverbs 15:23 (Voice) says, "There is great joy in having the right answer, and how sweet is the right word at the right time." Every situation isn't about *you* — but how you respond demonstrates God on the earth. The right response at the right time brings great joy!

In the midst of a challenge, God was using the moment to reveal Himself to an unbeliever. My response became a reflection of His joy in action.

> In the midst of a challenge, God was using the moment to reveal Himself to an unbeliever. My response became a reflection of His joy in action.

Truth be told, my goal wasn't to show God to my officemate. I was just trying to stay out of jail. *I AM gorgeous! Them hookers would devour me alive in prison.* Yasss! I said it!

Understanding the Power of Laughter

I had to learn two things from the Holy Spirit:

1. **Joy is my internal strength from God.** Laughter erupts from joy and becomes the demonstration of God's love. Challenges are invaluable opportunities to choose joy, let laughter break through, and allow God to shape my thoughts and influence my responses.

2. **I wasn't being personally attacked by my supervisor.** My anointed laugh disturbs the comfort of the spirits of unhappiness, despair, grief, and sorrow. So, the

enemy lashes out, trying to attack me and disrupt my joy. But I resist the devil — I *laugh* — and I watch him flee. I would rather disrupt *his* comfort!

A Scottish warrior once said, *"Dulcius Ex Asperis"* — *sweeter after difficulties*. You will certainly experience the sweetness of life after difficulties. Believe it or not, you were created for joy, and you have the ability to walk in it at any moment. People often ask me, 'How can you always be so happy or full of joy?' They think it's impossible. People actually think that I don't have challenges. But the truth is, God lives in me 24/7/365. He never leaves us; never forsakes us. It is not by my own strength (Zechariah 4:6), it is God's joy that fuels me. Laughter wells up in me as I write this. Honestly, that's just how I was created. I don't have a perfect explanation, it's simply who I am.

The ammunition of joy lifts heaviness, setting you and those around you free. Laugh out loud on purpose (*LOLP*) and live with ease.

Ammunition of Forgiveness

When forgiveness is used as a weapon, it becomes a defense in conflict, producing victory. Forgiveness is a subject that is not easy for us as humans to approach. It requires a level of passion and strength that we are not always willing to journey through. Honestly, forgiveness is challenging, but when we truly learn to forgive like God, we prevail and win in life. True forgiveness means reconciliation and restoration. When you operate in this kind of forgiveness, you restore a person back to their original position in your life — as if they NEVER did any wrong against you. Forgiveness removes all barricades that keep us from unity. This is what God does for us!

Fully exhausted, my mother would come home from work after being used and mistreated by life all day long. Her normal routine was to get out of the clothes that carried the stench of an unpleasant day and change into something more comfortable before reaching for her evening companions — Bacardi rum and marijuana. It seemed as if she was always trying to shake loose from something. Maybe she was trying to erase scars and bruises left by her own youth and divorce. Maybe I was a reminder of what was wrong in her life.

I was around 14, and on this particular afternoon, the drinking started early, and my mom was in another one of her episodes.

"I wish you were one of my abortions!" she suddenly blurted out.

I froze. "What?"

"You heard me," she slurred, her eyes filled with something unreadable. "I should have never had you."

Those words hit me like a wrecking ball at a construction site, tearing down any standing structure in its way. I could barely breathe. My chest tightened, and my vision blurred. Tears welled up in my eyes.

"I hate you!" I screamed as I turned and ran out of the room, my heart fully demolished. There was no chance of repair. No visible signs of life were left in me.

I laid on my bed with my head resting on a pillow drenched with violent tears. I must have cried the whole day. Those words began to dash through my mind like evening rush hour — racing through with no regard for the law. They only confirmed what I had feared all along, I would never be loved by my mother.

I cried so intensely that I felt like I was about to vomit. The nausea started in my belly and worked its way through my esophagus. My stomach clenched in pain. I jumped up, ran to the bathroom, lifted the toilet seat, and hung over the toilet bowl. Here it comes. I gagged. *Oh my gosh! What is happening?* Then, as if an involuntary expulsion, laughter burst forth from my innermost being.

That laughter went on for quite some time.

"What the hell is so funny?" my mom yelled from the other room. I put my hands over my mouth to try to keep the sound of laughter from escaping between my fingers into the atmosphere. *"Nothing,"* I muffled. But the laughter just continued to pour out of me. I lay on the bathroom floor, not understanding what was happening.

I didn't know who I could turn to for an explanation. There was no close friend to share this experience with — no one I thought would understand. Shoot, even I didn't understand. Looking back, I see it clearly: that laughter was a supernatural shield, keeping my heart from being completely shattered. It wasn't just an emotional response, it was a divine strategy, preparing me for a moment of healing I wouldn't experience until decades later.

The Crucial Courageous Conversation

More than 20 years later, I finally had that crucial courageous conversation with my mother regarding her harsh words. Seriously, folks, God is not uninformed about your life. Several months before, I had taken a training at work called "Crucial Conversations" — seriously, best training ever! The authors define a crucial conversation as a discussion between two or more people where the stakes are high, opinions vary, and emotions run strong. May I lovingly suggest that you take the training or get the book? I have applied the lessons learned at work and in my personal life.

I use the word *courageous* because one has to be brave regardless of the danger or high stakes. I had to push past my fear, my pride, and the anger that still tried to justify itself. I had to be more committed to healing than to holding on to hurt.

I decided to take the risk — approach an emotional topic and speak honestly without offense. I approached my mother with my story, but I was just as committed to hearing hers. It was time to collect the data I needed to finally get off that emotional, hurtful rollercoaster.

"Mom, you once told me that you wished I was one of your abortions. I felt rejected and unloved. What did you mean?"

I fully expected my mother to slap me into the middle of next week.

Unexpectedly, she grabbed me and began to cry. She let out a howl that could wake the dead. Her eyes were filled with embarrassment.

It was a difficult conversation that needed to happen, and it resulted in victory.

"That is a lie," she said. Looking me in the eyes, she states, "You are the best thing that ever happened to me."

We embraced each other like two love-struck teenagers, sobbing uncontrollably.

She softly whispered in my ear, "I love you, baby girl, and I will never say anything again that would cause you so much pain. Please forgive me."

I didn't wait for my mom to come to me to ask for forgiveness, I went to her because I was seeking unity. All those years ago, in that bathroom, God was supernaturally empowering me with a capability that would bring me to this very moment.

I Forgive You, Mom

I could literally feel my heart transforming, coming back to life. What was once demolished was now being reconstructed. That supernatural ability was the gift of laughter. Laughter had the vision to connect with forgiveness, restoring my mother back to her original position in my life as *my mother*. And to tell the truth, I was restored to my original position as her daughter. True forgiveness doesn't say, "I'll forgive but never forget." It says, "I choose to love you as if the hurt never happened."

The Call to Action

See God as your warrior and defender. Just because evil things are happening all around us doesn't negate the fact that God exists, and He cares for you personally.

> Forgiveness isn't passive, it's a choice to fight for unity.

Whatever external triggers try to defeat you — whether through words, wounds, or rejection — can be conquered.

If I had waited for my mother to come to me, I might still be waiting. Forgiveness isn't passive, it's a choice to fight for unity.

Who do you need to release today? What if laughter could be the very thing that opens the door to healing your relationships?

Ammunition of Praise

David, who authored much of the Psalms, truly understood how to praise God. Scripture even describes him as "a man after God's own heart" (1 Samuel 13:14). David pursued God with fervor and passion like a lovesick teenager in love for the very first time. He yearned to be close to God's heart. He expressed his love and devotion through songs and poetry, music, dance, and raw honesty — pouring out his joy, sorrow, and gratitude in every season of life.

Just as David's praise moved the heart of God, our laughter, when lifted in faith, becomes a force against the enemy. But laughter isn't just an expression of happiness; it's a weapon that shifts the atmosphere.

I've come to realize that human languages can never fully capture God's essence. No matter how eloquent our words, they fall short of describing His majesty. Yet, God doesn't demand perfection in our praise; He simply desires sincerity. He looks at the heart. Inspired by David's example and the joy-filled exhortations of Psalm 150, I incorporated laughter as a form of praise. Just as David praised God with music and dance, we too can lift up our hearts in joyous laughter, celebrating His goodness and boundless love.

> "Praise the Lord! Praise God in His sanctuary; praise Him in His mighty heavens! Praise Him for His acts of power; praise Him for His surpassing greatness! Praise

Him with the sound of laughter, celebrating His goodness and boundless love! Just as we praise Him with the trumpet, the harp, and the dance, let us also lift our hearts in joyous laughter. For laughter, like music, is from God — a unifying expression of His love and pleasure. Let everything that has breathe praise the Lord! Let every heart overflow with the sound of laughter in His presence. Praise the Lord!" (Psalm 150)

But what happens when life feels too heavy to praise? When trials press in, laughter may feel like the *last thing* we want to offer. Yet, that is when it becomes the most powerful.

When challenges arise, I lift my laughter as an offering of praise, redirecting all focus onto Jehovah. Praise flaunts His authority and sovereignty over every situation, even in the face of the enemy's temptations.

Sure, watching a funny movie or sharing a silly moment with family and friends brings joy to our lives. However, Ecclesiastes reminds us that there is a season and purpose for everything — including when and how we use our weapon of laughter. There's a time for a giggle, and there's a time for a deliberate, faith-filled belly laugh that shifts our mindset from:

- Anxiety to peace
- Worry to trust
- Grief to relief

- Doubt to belief

- Sorrow to hope

Through laughter, we resist temptation and live in the freedom God has promised.

Praise Your Way Through

Laughter, like praise, is an act of faith. It refuses to bow to fear or offense. When we laugh in faith, we are declaring: 'God, I trust You more than my emotions, my circumstances, and even my pain.'

The Bible is full of examples where praise wasn't just singing pretty songs — it was a strategy. Look at King Jehoshaphat in 2 Chronicles chapter 20. Surrounded by enemies and outnumbered, instead of sending his strongest warriors to the frontlines, he sent the Praise Team. As they began to worship, God confused the enemies so much they started taking each other out! That wasn't luck or coincidence, that was divine strategy — through praise. So, when you laugh as an act of praise, you're creating an atmosphere where God's presence can move, and the enemy cannot stand where God is moving.

When challenges arise, I lift my laughter as an offering of praise, redirecting all focus onto Jehovah. Spiritual warfare isn't won by impulse or wishful thinking — it requires intentional training, time, and repetition. Just as a soldier hones their skills before stepping onto the battlefield, we must prepare our minds and spirits, learning to effectively employ one of our most powerful weapons: laughter

When Praises Go Up

I remember the sting of her words as if they had been etched into my heart. A close friend, someone I deeply love and trusted, looked me in the eyes and said, "You need to learn to keep your mouth shut. Your opinion isn't needed."

Ouch.

The words hit harder than I expected. After all, she had *asked* for my opinion. Maybe she should have set some ground rules before inviting me to share my thoughts. But instead of clarifying, I kept my mouth shut, apologized, and moved on — or so I thought.

That night, as I lay in bed replaying the conversation, the hurt resurfaced. I felt small, silenced, and misunderstood. The enemy saw his opportunity, whispering lies, "Maybe she's right. Maybe you do talk too much. Maybe your voice really doesn't matter."

But then, something stirred in my spirit. I refused to let offense take root. Instead of dwelling on the hurt, I did something that made no logical sense — I laughed on purpose. Not just a small chuckle, but a full, uninhibited, joy-filled laugh of praise.

"God, You are still good! Ha! I refuse to let this steal my joy. Thank You for my voice. Thank You that my words have purpose. Thank You that even if others don't value what I say, You do!"

As I laughed, the heaviness lifted. The tension in my chest released. The more I laughed, the more I felt God's presence washing over me, reminding me that my voice was His gift. The enemy's attempt to silence me backfired, because instead of feeling defeated, I felt victorious. Instead of shrinking back, I stood firm. Instead of being weighed down, I soared.

That night, I learned something powerful: praise, even through laughter, disarms the enemy. It shifts the focus from pain to promise, from offense to freedom.

By the time I stopped laughing, I wasn't just smiling, I was free. The pain no longer had power over me. I had laughed my way into healing.

Choose Praise

So now, when discouragement tries to creep in, when someone's words cut deep, I remember I have a choice. I can stay wounded, or I can laugh my way into healing. And let me tell you, I choose laughter every time.

When I choose faith over fear and laughter over sorrow, my laughter becomes a weapon. It sends confusion into the enemy's camp, just as Judah's praise in 2 Chronicles 20.

Similarly, our laughter — rooted in faith and praise — dismantles the enemy's attacks and declares God's victory. Just like Judah, you too can walk away with the spoils of victory, your laughter declaring God's triumph over every battle.

Together, let's laugh boldly, laugh by faith, and watch as God turns our laughter into victory.

Take a moment right now — yes, right now! Think of a situation where you've felt defeated, then choose to laugh in faith. Speak victory over it and let your laughter declare that God is in control.

> "Thanksgiving will pour out of the windows; laughter will spill through the doors. Things will get better and better. Depression days are over. They'll thrive. they'll flourish. The days of contempt will be over." (Jeremiah 30:18-19 MSG)

This is what you will experience when you lift up laughter as praise.

Did you read that, depression days are over. Your laughter may bring you out of depression.

When laughter goes up, blessings come down.

In your own situation, how could the weapon of laughter replace your usual response and bring victory? How can you apply the ammunitions of love, joy, forgiveness, and praise in your life? These aren't just abstract ideas; they are powerful tools given by God to help you navigate challenges, heal wounds, and restore relationships.

Laughter shifts the atmosphere. Love conquers. Joy strengthens. Forgiveness frees. Praise elevates. The choice is yours. Will you allow these weapons to transform your life? The next time you face pain, rejection, or hardship, remember, you are not powerless. You are equipped to win.

Jehovah Gibbor Declaration Over for You

A message from God

I am Jehovah, your Father. In this season, you will know Me as Jehovah Gibbor — your Mighty Warrior, Powerful Champion, and Great Defender. I fight for you.

"The Lord is a warrior; the Lord is His name" (Exodus 15:3, NIV).

I, your God, declare this over you: I have never lost a battle, and because you are mine, you shall not lose. Every spirit of infirmity, shame, and oppression has been defeated in your life. My Word is true, and my promises are trustworthy. I see you, I stand with you, and I will never leave you.

Who is Jehovah Gibbor?

I am the Lord, armed and ready for battle — mighty and invincible in every way! (Psalm 24:8 (TPT))

I am your Rescuer. Your Safe Place. Your Defender.
With Me, there is no risk of failure — only victory. Everything you need flows from Me!

The wicked plot against you daily, but I laugh at their efforts — for they will not prevail (Psalm 2:4 (TPT)).

You are made in my image, so I declare this over you: You are my warrior.

I have trained your hands for war and given you the skills needed for battle (Psalm 144:1 (NKJV)).

So laugh!

Laugh, knowing you have already won.

Laugh, knowing victory is yours.

Laugh, because your joy is a weapon, and the enemy has already been defeated.

Stand firm, warrior. Laugh boldly. The battle is over — rejoice, for you have prevailed!

Let your laughter be your battle cry!!

Says the Lord.

Chapter 6:
Natural Gift with Supernatural Results

"I have the gift of laughter. I can make people laugh at will. In good times and in bad.

And that, I don't question. It was a gift from God."

— Buddy Hackett

During my first year at Humor Academy, we had to start a journal documenting our use of humor and laughter throughout the day. This was a challenge because laughter has always come naturally to me — I never had to think about it. But as I paid closer attention, I became more aware of how laughter shaped my interactions and responses to life.

My mom always said I was a natural entertainer, able to make people laugh at will. Keeping this journal helped me to discover something deeper: I am a *laugh artist*. I am here on earth to laugh out loud and paint a picture of transformation.

But of course, the enemy doesn't want you to know who you are, and he certainly doesn't want you to make an impact or draw people to Christ. Here come the challenges.

Understanding Your Natural Gift

Collins Dictionary defines a natural gift as an ability or skill someone is born with rather than one they have to learn. Laughter is exactly that — you don't have to learn it, but you do have to release it strategically.

As far back as I can remember, laughter has flowed like a river from the innermost parts of my being. It became my best friend, encouraging me to keep going and stay strong. But just because something is natural doesn't mean it doesn't need developing. I remember when God told me to learn my craft. That is when I started learning everything about laughter. We must become aware of our gifts and build the skills to operate in them.

Laughter in My DNA

Scientists may not be able to prove that laughter is written into our DNA, but that doesn't change the fact that God designed us with laughter in our framework.

I did some research on my ancestry and reconnected with a cousin on my father's side. As we talked, she told me how funny my father was. I started reminiscing about how he could walk into any room, and light would follow him. He was a storyteller, a joke-teller, and a natural entertainer. He didn't just make people laugh, he left them doubled over, slapping their knees, wiping tears from their eyes, and grabbing their stomachs in pure joy.

Now I see where I get it from. My father's DNA transmitted laughter genetics into the framework of my existence. He told dirty jokes and let's just say they are *way too nasty* to share in this book. But the heart of it remains: I was born with the natural gift of laughter. I can't outrun who I was created to be — and neither can you.

Discovering Your Own Natural Gift

Have you ever dismissed something natural about yourself, not realizing it was a gift from God? What have others said you do effortlessly? Maybe, like me, you've been walking in your gift all along, without even realizing it.

Want to understand your own natural gift? Here are a few steps to help:

- **Ask God.** He is always ready to reveal the truth about you. *He loves telling you stories about yourself!* You were already operating in your gift before you were sent to earth. (Read my chapter on "Laughter is a Calling.")

- **Ask others.** Your closest friends, family, and co-workers know you best. I once sent out a questionnaire asking people what they thought my superpower was — try it!

- **Identify what excites you.** What do you love doing but have pushed to the back of your mind? It's not about money, it's about impact. But trust me, if it's God's will, He will bless you through it.

For some, life has stolen their laughter. We've all suffered challenges or trauma. But your response to rough times determines whether you will overcome or be defeated.

Many of us dismiss our natural gifts for many reasons. Some are afraid to use their gifts because they fear criticism or judgment from others, or they worry about not being able to live up to their own expectations.

Know this — your natural gift isn't just for you; it's medicine. Yes, your gift is also a medicine for someone who desperately needs it. Just as my laughter creates healing spaces for others, your unique gift creates something in this world that would be missing without you.

Even if laughter isn't your specific gift, there's a parallel between how I reclaimed my laughter and how you can reclaim your natural gift. What voice, talent, or ability has been silent in you that needs to be released? What gift has the enemy tried to convince you is worthless or dangerous when released?

Like my laughter, your gift may be both a blessing and a weapon — bringing healing while simultaneously dismantling darkness.

The Battle Against Laughter

People struggle to believe that laughter can help them overcome. They assume that laughing means you are not taking life seriously. But laughter is not a distraction — it is a weapon. When the enemy sees you walking in joy, he will send people — strategically placed, diabolical distractions — to try and break you.

That's exactly what happened with my supervisor (a different supervisor than chapter 2).

I was at work and heading into my bi-weekly meeting with my supervisor. As I walked in, I responded with, "Yes, sir."

He closed the door behind him, looked me in the eye, and asked, "Did you just say 'Yes, massa?'"

I froze. *What?!*

The words hit me like a slap. Me, speechless? Impossible. My mind scrambled for clarity.

"What would make you think I would say such a thing?" I asked.

He shrugged and chuckled. "Uh, I don't know. I watched *Roots* last night."

Meeting over!

Let me be clear: this isn't about racism. It's about how the enemy uses every demonic attack to stop you from fulfilling your destiny. He is willing to do anything and use anyone to stop you in your tracks. Remember, the enemy has weapons too.

I already know how you would respond but I am not you.

I walked out of his office, heart pounding so loudly I could hear my own pulse. The HR office was only a few doors away, but the hallway suddenly felt miles long. Anger and shame weighed me down, slowing my steps. I stormed past HR, straight into the bathroom, and covered my mouth to stifle a scream.

I knew God was there. He always has a way of standing quietly, waiting for me to acknowledge Him. But I didn't feel like talking to Him. Instead, I wrestled with my own anger. "Does he see me as a slave? Am I not valuable? Was there an invisible line of hatred I had been unaware of?" I questioned myself.

I finally made it to HR to report what happened, but the process was long and exhausting. Victory was mine, but the enemy's real goal was to silence my laughter and steal my joy. So, he tried to distract me with racism.

Release Me

That night, I sat in my living room, physically exhausted but mentally unable to rest as the day's events replayed in my mind. Even as I ignored the TV, my thoughts couldn't escape the encounter. Eventually, my body surrendered to sleep, but my spirit was still wrestling. I had a dream that felt more real than reality itself, I found myself back in my living room when a dark shadow appeared.

My giant Goliath arrived, uninvited, flanked by his old crew — shame, sorrow, and fear. They strutted toward me like long-lost friends, grinning as if they had a right to be here. I had evicted them before, but here they were, bold enough to see if I'd let them move back in.

I recognized them instantly. You never forget the ones who once held you captive.

With wicked delight, they yanked my laughter from me and threw her at my feet.

"Things ain't so funny now, huh?" one sneered.

Then they collapsed onto their backs like dead roaches, legs kicking in the air, high-fiving each other as they howled with laughter. Thinking they had won.

"C'mon, girl. Laugh. Laugh! We dare you."

Their voices echoed in my mind, their shadows looming over me.

"You're nothing."

"No one cares about you."

"You will never be free."

"God can never use someone like you"

I grew disheartened. Powerless. Depressed. Unimportant.

Sound familiar? Have these voices tried to creep into your life too? Have they whispered lies that made you question your worth, your purpose, or your strength?

But worst of all?

I wasn't laughing.

Thank God I woke up. But that dream haunted me. I couldn't seem to shake the effects of its torment. A few weeks later, I was at the point of just giving up. I desperately prayed. God, why did You allow this?

A few weeks later, I had another dream. I was at a comedy club, laughing so hard that I doubled over in delight. I couldn't stop laughing. At my table sat Laughter with a note that said, "Release me."

I woke up still laughing. It was as if my dream had collided with reality. I couldn't stop laughing! Suddenly, His voice broke through, rushing in like a sprinter crossing the finish line. Before I could react, He surrounded me, wrapping me in His presence.

"Nandi, my sweet one... don't be afraid. I am your Lord God Almighty."

I exhaled, relief washing over me. "Daddy ... I'm so glad You're here. I've been waiting for You."

"I know," He said gently. "I've been here all along."

His presence felt so close, so reassuring.

"You have to know that I am always with you," said the Almighty. "Always.

"Listen to Me when I say this: You are free to laugh. It is in you to laugh. Have I not called you Laughter to the Nations? Your laughter is medicine — it will bring healing, dispel depression, and break the grip of dis-ease," He continued. "This is who you are. This is what I have spoken over you."

Tears welled in my eyes. I could feel His love, His power, His truth.

"I am always with you, sweetie. Be courageous. Be strong," God said. "Now... go look up the definition of laughter."

My hands trembled as I reached for my iPad. It felt like this wasn't just a casual suggestion — it was a doorway to go deeper. I'd heard the word "laughter" my entire life, had experienced it countless times, but had I ever truly understood what it meant at its core. I became curious.

As I typed "definition of laughter" into the search bar, I knew I was about to unlock revelation knowledge that had been hiding in plain sight. The screen loaded, and there it was — simple words that suddenly carried the understanding of my destiny.

"To be of the kind that inspires joy."

Wow.

I read it again, letting each word sink deep into my spirit. Not just to experience joy, but to inspire it. Not just to laugh, but to be the catalyst for laughter in others. Not just a momentary emotion, but a kind of person — a being whose very nature brings joy to life around them.

"This is what I have called you to do, sweetie," my Father whispered, and everything was settled in my heart.

Natural Gift, Supernatural Results

Nothing catches God by surprise. That night, I stepped fully into who I was created to be — of the kind that inspires joy. I didn't wait for someone else to encourage me. I became my own motivation, my own source of praise.

I lifted my voice in laughter — loud, unapologetic, explosive. This time, it was intentional. It wasn't just laughter; it was warfare. It pierced the atmosphere, breaking through every weight that had tried to silence me.

From that moment on, I didn't care who it offended. My laughter was a sound of freedom, a weapon of praise, a declaration of victory. God let me laugh again, and I raised the roof with shouts of joy.

Job 8:20-22 states, "He will once again fill your mouth with laughter and your lips with shouts of joy" (NLT).

I decided to choose laughter and joy. So, I laughed over and over and over and over. I couldn't stop because I was experiencing breakthrough.

I will never stop laughing, no matter how much I am tested.

Because now, I understand.

The enemy fought so hard to steal my laughter because he was terrified of me. He saw what I didn't — my personality, my anointing, my power of influence. He knew that if I ever realized just how powerful I am, I would impact others and lead them to their own breakthrough.

And worst of all? He knew that my laughter — my natural gift — would become a missile against the kingdom of darkness. The gift that I was born with became a supernatural gift.

The joke is on the devil. It is written in Psalm 37:13, "Bad guys have it in for the good guys, obsessed with doing them in. But God isn't losing any sleep; to Him, they're a joke with no punchline" (MSG). Even God laughs at the enemy — because in the end, the enemy's schemes are powerless against His sovereignty!

He thought his plans would destroy me, but God flipped the script. What was meant for my downfall, God used for my good.

"You intended to harm me, but God intended it all for good. He brought me to this position so I could save the lives of many people" (Genesis 50:20, NLT).

A comic's job is to make you laugh for a temporary moment. However, laughter is my position. It's not just for a few laughs, it's for saving lives.

> "You intended to harm me, but God intended it all for good. He brought me to this position so I could save the lives of many people"

What are *you* called to do? It, too, is meant to save lives.

Laughter confirms our faith. It shuts down worry. It destroys anxiety.

It strengthens us from the inside out.

So now? I laugh boldly. I triumph loudly.

And I WIN.

And just like that, I knew, I had won that battle. I looked up, and there she was… my old friend, Laughter, waiting for me. She sat on the edge of my bed, chains broken, strong and tall. She held a sign that simply read: "Thank you." And as I watched, that sign transformed into a fiery sword.

Laughter — my defender, my protector.

I will never let you be kidnapped and bound again!

I release the sound of my laughter into the atmosphere, shattering every barrier that dares to stand in my way.

What about you?

What will *you* do to set your laughter free — so it will never be bound again?

To be of the Kind that Inspires Joy

Laughter is my natural gift, but God's grace makes it supernatural. The enemy fought so hard to stop me because he knew how powerful I was. He wanted me to doubt my influence, but my laughter is a weapon against darkness.

The next day at work, I was in my office laughing with a coworker. Then she said, "Welcome back."

"Uh… what?" I asked.

"It's good to hear you laugh again. The office felt lifeless without it."

"Wow," I thought. "I get it now, God. I am onboard with Your vision."

Now, what about you? The enemy wants to steal your laughter because he fears its power. What will you do to reclaim it?

Put this book down for five minutes and JUST LAUGH. I dare you.

Chapter 7:
When Laughter Becomes a Message

"I will release the spirit and power of my laughter and joy in the earth, and healing will invade the hearts of men."

– (Prophetic word from God)

A few years ago, I was sitting in church and during worship, I had come to a point where I became completely involved with pursuing the presence of God. Closing my eyes, I soon forgot where I was as the sounds of human worship and music of adoration had become aloof. I searched the rooms of my own heart seeking the One I love.

All of a sudden, a woman laughing caught my attention. My human existence caught up with my moment of hot pursuit. I was unwilling to open my eyes, but this woman's laughter was loud and unrelenting. It seemed as if she couldn't stop. I wanted to turn around and see who it was, but I sat frozen like an ice cube. Her laughter magnified in my spirit to where I could literally hear the voice of the Holy Spirit coming from this woman's laughter.

"I hear the cries of my beloved children," I heard God say. *"I will begin to release the spirit of and the power of my laughter and joy in the earth and cause healing to invade the hearts of men."*

"WOOOO!!! What?!?!?! Wait a minute," my thoughts were loud.

I questioned if that was really the Holy Spirit. Was that really God?

But before I could fully embrace the moment, another voice barged in, unwelcome.

"Ohhh, you really think that was God, huh?" Doubt snickered, circling me like a vulture. "You, of all people? You actually believe you heard God's voice through that woman's laughter?"

Then it cackled, loud and cruel.

"HAHAHAHAHAHA! That is ridiculous," the doubt in my mind sneered at me. "That's not even in the Bible. You should just get up and leave church right now before anyone figures out how crazy you are. Matter of fact, come on over to the dark side — we could use a good girl like you."

My heart sank.

I probably should have left, because I didn't hear a single word my pastor said for the rest of the service.

I blinked, snapping back to reality.

"I love you in Jesus' name," someone said, wrapping me in a hug. "See you at Bible Study!" Wait. What? Service was over? Just like that. Had I really been in a fog the whole time? Doubt had robbed me of an entire message.

Panic set in. I needed answers. Without hesitation, I started pushing my way through the crowd, desperate, determined, just like the woman with the issue of blood. I frantically ran up to my pastor.

"I really need to talk with you," I said. "Really, really, really, really, really need to talk with you." I was like a child that had to pee and couldn't hold it any longer.

He looked at me and was silent for a moment. I don't know if he could see on my face exactly what I was experiencing in my heart. Thank God he answered when he did. "Sure, let's go to my office."

When God Calls you to More

We stepped into his office, and before I could even sit down, my pastor motioned toward a glass of water.

"Have a seat, daughter. Do you need something to drink?"

"No, thank you."

He raised an eyebrow. "Are you sure? You look like you need something to drink."

"OMG. I am not thirsty, dude!" But instead of saying that, I forced a polite, "No, sir, I'm good."

He nodded slowly. "Okay… so tell me what's going on?"

I jumped up out of my seat.

"I AM A DEVIL!! HELP!"

His face? Completely unreadable.

I started ranting like a lunatic. "How does this work? Do you cast it out? Do we need to get some oil? Shouldn't you get some backup?!"

He sat there, calm and unbothered but I know he was secretly scanning the room for his escape plan. (I would have.)

Then, in a stern but fatherly voice, he said, "Sit down and tell me what is wrong."

I let out a deep, frustrated sigh and slumped into the chair.

"I GOT A DEVIL IN ME! HOW DO WE GET HIM OUT?"

To my surprise, he didn't even flinch. "Why do you think you have a devil?" he asked.

I explained everything — how I heard what I thought was the Holy Spirit speaking through a woman's laughter, and since I never read anything like that in the Bible, then obviously… I must have a devil.

He stared at me. The look on his face said, 'Yep, this chick is off her rocker.'

But when he finally spoke, it wasn't what I expected.

"Tell me exactly what you heard."

I took a breath.

"I hear the cries of My beloved children. I will begin to release the spirit and power of My laughter and joy in the earth and cause healing to invade the hearts of men."

A silence fell over the room. It felt eternal.

Finally, he exhaled. "Wow… that is beautiful."

I blinked. "Wait… what? Beautiful?"

"First of all," he said, "you don't have a devil. Besides, the devil would never tell you something that is encouraging and beautiful."

I stared at him, still unsure.

"Maybe I've never heard of anyone interpreting someone's laughter before," he admitted. "But listen, Nandi, God can do anything He wants because He is God. If He can use a donkey to speak and change someone's life, surely He can use you to interpret laughter and change the course of mankind."

His eyes locked onto mine. "God is not in a box. But we put Him in one because of our limited thinking."

Then he smiled.

"I also recognize something else about you, you have the ability to change the atmosphere with your laughter." He leaned in. "But hear me, daughter. God can't use you unless you show up."

Then, with a knowing grin, he added, "So, show up."

God's laughter in the Earth

My spiritual father prayed a release of anointing to walk in the call of God on my life. That day I gained more confidence in God and what He had put on the inside of me. I realized that we struggle with hearing God's voice because we think it should look a particular way or have a particular sound. I have decided to take God out of that box and let Him fully express in His own way. Express in His own way through me.

After talking with my pastor and praying, the Holy Spirit led me to read Psalms 126:6. "They may weep as they go out carrying their seed to sow, but they will return with *joyful laughter* and shouting with gladness as they bring back armloads of blessing and a harvest overflowing" (TPT).

I want to encourage you by the power of the Holy Ghost. God has a message for you. Presently there are great waves of mourning and sorrow sweeping across our country. He sees the tears you cry. You have been sowing seeds of tears and prayers. Some of us have been so hurt that we have been crying for years. You have been under so much pressure. You have gone to the altar carrying your seeds and sowing in tears.

STOP WEEPING. STOP CRYING. GOD HAS HEARD YOU!

"I have heard the cries of my children," says the Lord. Your cries (prayers) have reached the very heart of God and penetrated His very being. He promises to release boundless surges of laughter and joy that will free you from all you are concerned about. God's spirit of laughter and joy will step into your life and transform you suddenly.

I pronounce a blessing that you will be saturated, drenched, and become soaking wet with the power of the Holy Spirit to laugh yourself silly as you carry armloads of blessings. You will be filled with God's joy and laughter that you will escape the clutch of your enemy. You will experience a harvest overflowing in your life. You are empowered by God for every situation and circumstance. Health is restored to your bones. Your children serve the Lord happily. Your marriage has Dunamis power. You have wholesome relationships. You have favor on your job. Your relationship with God is dynamic. Stand strong in the power of God and He will empower you to prosper in every area of your life.

The very act of laughing causes your inner man to gird up with strength and power. You are NOT just laughing haphazardly, you are activating the anointing of laughter by the power of the Holy Spirit to snatch your soul (your mind, will, and emotions) out of darkness into God's marvelous light.

Laugh boldly. Laugh freely. Laugh, knowing that heaven is rejoicing over you. Your breakthrough has already begun.

Chapter 8:
Her Name is Laughter: The Prophetic Power of Identity

"To the one who is victorious, I will give that person a white stone with a new name written on it, known only to the one who receives it."

— Revelation 2:17

This chapter was not easy to write. For a while, it felt misplaced — like it didn't quite belong in this book. I wrestled with the words, second-guessed their purpose, and questioned the connection between my name and the message of laughter. But deep down, I knew there was something there — something meaningful, something divine. It just hadn't revealed itself yet.

What unfolded in this chapter is more than a story about how I got my name. It's a revelation about identity, purpose, commitment, legacy, and how even the things we dismiss — like a name we didn't choose — can be filled with purpose from the heart of God.

> "Fear not, for I have redeemed you; I have called you by your name; you are Mine"

Isaiah 43:1 says, "Fear not, for I have redeemed you; I have called you by your name; you are Mine" (NKJV).

I love this scripture because it reminds us that God personally selects and calls us by name – it is not random but intentional. We were chosen, selected, and named for a specific assignment that only we can accomplish.

God was unveiling another layer of my individuality. He led me on a transformational journey of discovering Nandi Louise.

Before diving into my story, let me say this: Even if your name doesn't seem to match your personality or purpose, God still calls you by name and anointed you with a purpose.

Your name may have come from your parents, but your identity comes from God. When He speaks your name, it contains power, purpose, and destiny. Honestly, it also reveals your character.

At first, I could not see how my name connected to my calling. But the more I listened to God, the more I realized: Your name describes you, and aligns you. It's heaven's way of announcing your identity to the world.

Alignment With Your Name

We live in a world where identity is based on your driver's license, your social security, your zip code, your credit score. But none of those things truly tell the story of who you are. They may validate your existence in a world system, but they don't substantiate who you are in the kingdom of God.

I used to think names were just... names; labels. Something we respond to, but not something that revealed destiny. But God began showing me that my name bared my character and destiny. They are how people identify us — they're how He identifies us. The Bible states that you shall know them by their fruit (character).

In many cultures around the world, children are named with great intention — not just for how the name sounds, but for the meaning behind it. When parents choose names, they believe those names would shape their character and future.

And when you begin to understand what He calls you — not what the world has called you — something begins to shift inside.

My name aligns with my purpose and character. I now have confidence in myself, my calling, and in God.

Names carry a frequency (in the atmosphere) that ignites alignment with God's plan for His Kingdom. What is your name? If you don't know it, you're living misaligned with who you truly are. If God has called you by name, stop agreeing with the names the enemy whispers over your life.

Your name is *not* rejected, unwanted, whore, tainted, shameful, or useless. They don't belong to you. Break the agreement with the enemy's names. Come into agreement with the name God has spoken over you and align with your Kingdom identity and destiny.

God knows your name. He's calls you *chosen, beloved, redeemed, anointed, set apart*. That's your real name, your Kingdom identity.

My identity is prophetic. It's extremely important, especially considering where our country is heading in this season. We are falling deeper into depression and fear. I am a reminder that the Joy of the Lord is your strength and can bring about wholeness.

In a time where culture is confused about identity, God is restoring clarity. Knowing who you are — and what He calls you — matters more than ever.

Names Carry Power

Throughout history, names carried power; they were declarations of distinction. Parents declared who their children would become, speaking character and destiny through the name they gave. Many cultures name their children based on:

- Events surrounding their birth
- Emotions or warnings
- Misfortune
- Famous people
- Family traditions
- Cars or flowers
- And sometimes… just because it *sounds nice!*

Sorrow to Strength

Let's start with the story of Jabez in 1 Chronicles 4:9–10. His name literally means "sorrow" because his mother bore him in pain. Imagine that — your name being a daily reminder of someone else's grief.

But Jabez didn't settle for what he was named. He cried out to God and prayed a bold prayer that changed everything. "Oh that You would bless me and enlarge my territory! Let your hand be with me, and keep me from harm so that I will be free from pain," and God answered him.

His story shows us something profound: just because you were named in pain doesn't mean you were destined to live in it.

God reversed what was spoken over him.

I can't help but laugh! God turned his sorrow into his greatest strength. Divine Alignment! His territory was, indeed, expanded (not just land but also his influence). Yay!

If Jabez, can pray it, so can I. Father God, keep me from harm so that I will be free from pain. I declare a new mindset over us today. I decree that the frequency of our names comes into alignment with the Kingdom of God. No more sorrow. I only identify with Kingdom names – only Heaven's identity. Amen.

Everyone Will Laugh

God didn't just redeem sorrow — He also forgave disbelief to ensure His plans would prevail. Abraham and Sarah are a perfect example of how names can reflect a family's purpose. God changed both their names to align with their destiny: to give birth to a nation.

Let's look at Sarah's story in Genesis chapters 18 and 19. When she overheard God telling Abraham she would have a child, she laughed — of course she did! She was nearly 90, and he was pushing 100!

But God kept His promise, and when their baby was born, they named him Isaac, which means "he laughs," in Hebrew.

Then Sarah said in Genesis 21:6, "God has graced me with the gift of laughter! To be sure, everyone who hears my story will laugh with me."

Yass, Sarah! I'm laughing with you, girl. Thank God He graced you with laughter — because that is *way* too old to be having somebody's baby! But you were graced for the calling.

See, God always speaks with purpose. He saw their future, not their present limitations.

Isn't that powerful? The very thing she once laughed at in doubt, she later laughed through in victory.

Your name doesn't just carry meaning — it can carry a testimony.

Even Jesus' Name Carried Destiny

And if names are important, how much more did they matter in the life of Jesus? His name was not random — it was prophecy wrapped in purpose.

Jesus' name was a declaration of His destiny. His name fully aligned with his calling and purpose.

The angel told Joseph, "You shall call His name Jesus, for He will save His people from their sins" (Matthew 1:21).

His name literally means "Savior" — and He fulfilled His purpose perfectly. Thank God, because of Jesus, I have been saved from my sins and redeemed from everything.

Just as Jesus' name declared His mission, our names proclaim our mission too. As Jesus is, so are we (1 John 4:17).

My parents may not have realized it, but God made sure I was named Nandi — because laughter would be my calling. My calling grants me access to make laughter footprints in the earth and stomp on every serpent, in Jesus' name.

How I Got My Name

But here's the truth — my parents didn't put that much thought into naming me. No deep revelation. No prophetic vision. No divine encounter. Actually, they left the decision to my Auntie.

She was an educator who traveled to Africa many times for study, and on one of her trips, she returned with a list of African names. According to history (*okay, according to my momma, so you know its official*), after reviewing the list of names, my parents chose Nandi. Their choice was not based on its deep meaning, special significance, or divine revelation; nope.

It was simply the easiest to spell and pronounce.

HaHaHaHaHaHaHa. Are you laughing out loud just a little? Because I sure did! That's it, no grand intention, no prophetic moment, no deep purpose. It's just easy to spell and pronounce!

No Coincidence, Just Providence

Let me tell you, Nandi is NOT easy to pronounce. But despite my parents' simple reasoning, their choice was no accident. What looked like a random decision was actually God orchestrating my identity. The Holy Spirit was at work ensuring that my earthly name would align with my personality and my calling.

Because when God names something, He names it with purpose.

This girl named Nandi would grow up to bring laughter, joy, and strength to God's people. She came to be filled with the Holy Spirit, laughter, and joy, even in her mother's womb.

Defining Moment

The big reveal.

My name is Nandi, I was named after Queen Nandi, known as the mother of Shaka - King of the Zulu Nation. She was known as a mother of warriors. Queen Nandi's story hails her as a strong, confident leader and a warrior.

My name means sweet one, a woman of high esteem, and strong willed; to be happy, joyous, jubilant, and satisfied. It also means to always be filled with excitement and joy.

People who know me would say that definition fits me like a snug glove. Now I am truly walking in the character and power of my name.

Turns out, that one day, my story too would hail me as a strong confident leader and a warrior. But my father (God) wasn't done.

One day, He told me to look up – this time – the meaning of my middle name. I don't like my middle name, so I wasn't a fan of looking it up. Being obedient, I did as instructed and looked up the meaning of Louise, my middle name.

Here's what I found: "Renowned warrior or fighter." It also means strength, courage, and a spirit of standing one's ground.

I had a close friend who loved to call me Weezie – yes, as in the Jeffersons (no, you cannot; don't even think about it). Ewww. Haha!

Everything God creates, He names.

And Nandi Louise? That is my God-given identity and purpose. I am a strong willed, joyous, confident warrior - all from the heart of God.

As I began to understand the meaning behind my name, God continued to confirm its prophetic significance in unexpected ways.

A Prophetic Confirmation

When I was five years old, my auntie wrote a poem about me — one that was unmistakably prophetic about who I was meant to be in the earth.

Young girl child, who brought laughter
Nandi; O bringer of Joy
O prompter of Care
Nandi; Reminder of Responsibility
May you learn the Word
Use it wisely, oh use the Word wisely.

Did you catch that?

My name was already declaring my purpose before I even knew who I was. That poem was a confirmation of the prophecy that had been written in God's heart long before I was born.

And here's what I've learned: You can't outrun who God says you are. No matter where life takes you, your identity will always call you back to purpose.

Why Identity Matters

Yes, this was one of the hardest chapters for me to write. For weeks, I struggled. Why did this chapter feel disconnected from the rest of my book? Why did it feel like my name had no connection with laughter?

Then, the Holy Spirit spoke to my heart, "Your name isn't just a name. It's a calling. It is the very fabric of who you are."

Your identity matters.

It defines you. It validates you.

Consider this: the biggest international crime today is identity theft. People go to extreme lengths to steal someone's identity. So does the enemy! But what really keeps the enemy up at night isn't your money — it's your identity in Christ.

The enemy wants to keep you blind to who you truly are, because when you know who you are and whose you are, his grip on your destiny weakens.

A Question to Ponder

Your name isn't an accident. Even if it was picked out of a hat, chosen because it was easy to spell, passed down from a family tradition, or named after a car — God still knew it. He saw it. He approved it.

And if your name doesn't seem to match your personality or purpose, don't worry — He has another one. God renamed me Laughter to the Nations, He can rename you. (Revelations 2:17)

When you begin to walk in the power of your identity, heaven responds. Doors open. Chains break. Destiny begins to unfold.

Her name is laughter — a prophetic sound.

Her identity is joy.

Her destiny is calling.

So, after reading this chapter, I want you to ask yourself:

Can a person's name determine their destiny? Define their purpose? Shape their character?

Take a moment; sit with this.

The name Nandi Louise has influence over my destiny, purpose, and character. I needed to share this story, because it's the blueprint for what I am creating in this world. It's the foundation of my true identity.

Just like God ensured my name aligned with my calling and personality, He has done the same for you. You are not here by accident. Your name, your purpose, and your destiny were spoken by God long before you arrived on this earth. Take this journey of discovery with Him, as He has something powerful to reveal to you.

Reflection & Identity Exercise

God is intentional with names. He knew you before you were born, and your name carries meaning. Now, it's time for you to explore your own identity.

Step 1: Look Up Your Name

- Research the meaning of your first name.
- Write down what it means in different cultures or languages.
- If you were named after someone, what was their story?

Step 2: Seek God's Perspective

- Ask God, "Father, how does my name connect to my purpose?"

- Reflect on whether your name aligns with your personality.
- If your name doesn't seem to fit, ask God, "What do You call me?" He will tell you – that is how I got the name "Laughter to the Nations."

Step 3: Declare Your Identity

- **Write a declaration** about who you are in Christ. Use the definitions you found in your research.

Example: Declaration of Identity

I am Nandi — named with purpose, called by God.
Before I took my first breath, He spoke my name and declared my destiny.
I am not an accident. I am not overlooked. I am divinely chosen.

God has filled me with joy, strength, and laughter; and I walk boldly in my calling.
My sound of my laughter matters. My presence carries purpose. My laughter is a weapon.

The enemy cannot steal my identity, silence my laughter, or dim my light.
I am who God says — a warrior, a bringer of joy, a daughter of the King.

I will live out my purpose with faith and confidence, knowing that I am fully seen, fully loved, and fully equipped for His glory.

In Jesus' name, Amen.

Conclusion:
But Not the End

The ministry (service to God and people) of laughter is a powerful and often overlooked part of our spiritual walk, and our spiritual warfare. Too often, it's treated as entertainment, a light-hearted escape. But laughter, God's burst of joy, was always part of His design to destroy the works of the devil.

Yes, the enemy comes to steal, kill, and destroy. But Jesus said He came to destroy the works of the devil. And guess what? Laughter is part of Jesus' divine strategy.

So here's the question:

Is laughter the superhero we've been overlooking?

Can it rescue us from chaos, disasters, despair, and deception? Can it be used as a tool for wholeness? A weapon of joy? A defense to defeat sin?

Absolutely.

There is a spirit realm in full operation. Our inability to see it with human eyes doesn't make it less real. Similarly, Jesus spoke on the wind — it blows where it wishes, and you hear the sound of it, but cannot tell where it comes from and where it goes (John 3:8). Not seeing it does not negate its existence, nor its behavior.

As believers, we've been equipped with a divine toolbox — spiritual weapons, tools, and heavenly resources designed to help us overcome. But there's one tool many have forgotten... or never even discovered: Laughter.

You were born with the ability to laugh. It's not something you had to learn; you were born with laughter; it's already inside you and a part of your emotional makeup. And here's the secret: something doesn't have to be funny for you to laugh. That's what I call intentional laughter — laughing on purpose to break through heaviness, unlock supernatural joy, and walk in freedom.

So now the question is: Will you use it? Will you pick up the weapon of laughter, put it to work, and let it transform your life?

The choice is yours. Remember, laughter has always been within you. It's time to let it do what it was created to do.

Strategies to Activate the Ministry of Laughter

Strategy 1: Start Your Day with Joyful Praise

Laughter as Worship

Begin each morning with laughter as an act of worship, setting the tone for a joyful and faith-filled day.

How to Implement:

- Spend 5–10 minutes laughing intentionally, even if it feels awkward at first. Think of a funny memory, watch something silly, or just laugh at the wonder of waking up alive.

- Meditate on Nehemiah 8:10, "The joy of the Lord is your strength."

- Declare with boldness:

Today is the day You have made, and I will rejoice and be glad in it. I choose to laugh with God! My laughter is a declaration of faith, a weapon of strength, and an act of worship. I thank You, Lord, for this day, and I trust You with whatever comes my way. Even when it's challenging, I will not be shaken. Joy is my choice, and laughter is my gift from You. I have wisdom. My heart is light, my spirit is strong, and my day is filled with divine joy. In Jesus' name, Amen.

Strategy 2: Take Laughter Breaks

Laughter as a Time Out

Use laughter as a breather throughout the day to combat stress, anxiety, and negative thoughts.

How to Implement:

- Set reminders to take "laughter breaks" 2–3 times a day.
- During each break, laugh intentionally (even at your frustrations) to release tension and reclaim joy.
- When overwhelmed, sit up straight, take a deep breath, and laugh on purpose. Invite God's peace to flood in.
- Declaration:

When I feel overwhelmed, I choose to laugh with intention! My laughter releases stress, clears my mind, and unlocks divine creativity. I invite the Holy Spirit into my space — He fills me with peace, clarity, and focus. I am productive, I am strong, and I overcome every challenge with joy!

In Jesus' name, Amen.

Strategy 3: End Your Day with Laughter

Laughter as Reflection

Wind down by finding humor in your day and giving thanks for God's grace — especially when the day was hard.

How to Implement:

- Spend 5 minutes before bed recalling something funny, silly, or unexpected from your day.
- If the day was tough, laugh anyway, knowing God was with you through it all.
- Meditate on James 1:2–4, "Count it all joy…"
- Nighttime Prayer:

Heavenly Father, at the end of this day, I choose to laugh at my mistakes and rest in Your grace. I am not perfect, but I am deeply loved. Thank You for guiding me, strengthening me, and reminding me that joy is my inheritance. No matter what today held, I trust that tomorrow is a new day, filled with fresh mercy and endless possibilities. In Jesus' name, Amen.

Final Thoughts

Alongside reading your Bible, prayer, and worship, add laughter. Every day. On purpose. With purpose. You'll begin to laugh from the inside out — not just in response to life, but as a powerful, intentional act of faith, healing, and joy.

Laughter will find its place in the world again.

It is my mission to ensure that laughter finds it's place. Our world — not just this country, but globally — is spiraling deeper into sin and drifting from the presence of God. Yet in the midst of all this darkness, we carry a joy that cannot be explained and a light that cannot be dimmed.

Apostle Paul reminds us in 2 Corinthians 4:8–9 (Voice):

"We are cracked and chipped from our afflictions on all sides, but we are not crushed by them. We are bewildered at times, but we do not give in to despair. We are persecuted, but we have not been abandoned. We have been knocked down, but we are not destroyed."

Paul understood despair. He lived through persecution, pain, pressure, and heartbreak — and yet he held on.

Acts 16:25 describes Paul in prison — praying, and praising. They were celebrating in the middle of the night that sparked an earthquake that shook the foundation of their persecution. Doors flew open. Chains broke.

I had to learn to praise God for my trails instead of crying about them. When I chose laughter over despair, chains started breaking in my own life – freedom began to show up.

You and I face troubles every day. The enemy is strategic in his attacks. His goal is simple: to wear you down and wear you out.

He comes with depression, suicidal thoughts, fear, confusion, and mental fatigue. His intention is to apply just enough pressure to make you:

- Faint (feel feeble and weak)
- Grow weary (sink into depression)
- Become exhausted (emotionally shattered and spiritually tired)
- Lose consciousness (forget who you are in Christ)

- Misplace your awareness (detach from reality)
- Shrink back from your purpose

But the devil is a liar.

Jesus tells us in John 10:10: "The thief comes only to steal, kill, and destroy. But I came that you may have life and have it more abundantly."

The enemy wants your focus — he wants you consumed with what *he's* doing so you'll forget what God has already done.

He wants to convince you that God isn't who He says He is. But let me remind you: God is the one and only Living God - faithful. His Word is true, and His joy is your strength. When the storm is raging, I keep laughing and holding on to my Daddy.

There is a Latin phrase I hold close to my heart: *Incepto ne desistam* – "May I not shrink from my purpose."

Let that be your affirmation. Let it echo louder than fear, disappointment, or discouragement.

Declare that over yourself right now. Say it aloud. Let's agree — here and now — that we will not allow the enemy's tactics to keep us from our calling, our joy, or our purpose. May I not shrink (withdraw, pull back, decrease, dry up, diminish) from my purpose.

A Prayer of Activation

I declare right now that every time you laugh, the anointing of God is released like a weapon of mass destruction — disarming the fiery darts of the enemy and shattering the lies that have tried to attach themselves to your mind, your soul, and your destiny.

May my laughter rise like holy fire, tearing down strongholds of despair, breaking through walls of hopelessness, silencing the voice of self-criticism, and healing the deep wounds of trauma that have lingered for far too long.

I decree that the sound of my laughter is not just a reaction — it is a *revelation*. A sound from heaven that confuses the camp of the enemy and sends demons fleeing in terror. My laughter is disruptive. My laughter is prophetic. My laughter is one of the strongest weapons in war.

I send forth the weapon of laughter now — like a divine bomb into every dark place the enemy has tried to build a fortress. May every plot, plan, scheme, and strategy of hell be burned up by the holy joy of the Lord rising within me.

Let the oil of gladness drip from my spirit and overflow into my home, my relationships, my calling, my workplace, and my mind. Let joy be my shield, and let laughter be my sword.

Every obstacle standing in my way is demolished in the name of Jesus.

Every oppressive thought is uprooted. Every heavy spirit is lifted. Every ounce of fear is cast out. And every delay is broken. Now.

May I rise in boldness, walk in wholeness, and laugh with holy confidence — knowing the joy of the Lord is not just my strength… it is my *superpower*.

In the mighty, matchless, miracle-working name of Jesus, Amen and Agreed!

Daily Dose of Laughter Confessions

The Power of Our Words

Your words are so powerful that they will kill or give life, and the talkative person will reap the consequences.

— Proverbs 18:21 (Easy-to-Read Version)

The Power of Our Words: No More Delay

The experience of encountering God can be amazing, sometimes strange, and even unfamiliar. How we experience Him differs from person to person, but one thing remains constant: God never changes. This particular encounter with Him was unlike any I'd ever had before. It was so vivid, so real, that even now, I still wonder — was I dreaming or awake?

A Visitation Like No Other

I remember sitting at my kitchen table, meditating on my life, envisioning my ministry through God's eyes. As I sat there, I could sense the Holy Spirit's presence growing stronger, filling the space around me. Something inside me stirred, a strange sensation deep in my belly. It felt like a rumbling, a churning, something powerful brewing within me.

Then — something happened.

A jolt shot through me, as if something deep inside had been awakened. Before I knew it, my mouth opened but instead of words, flaming swords shot out with incredible force! These fiery swords zipped across the room, bouncing off the walls like they had a mind of their own. They moved with such speed and intensity, I barely had time to react. I ducked, hands over my head, trying not to get sliced up by my own words!

And then, something even more extraordinary happened. The flaming swords began to shift and transform, morphing before my very eyes. They became words. Not just ordinary words — living, breathing, moving words.

I blinked in disbelief. "What is going on?" I yelled. The fiery words drew closer to me, and one phrase took shape: "No More Delay."

Then, to my utter shock, the word "Delay" spoke.

Conversation with Delay

"I am Delay," it said, its voice smooth but unsettling. "I've been lying dormant, hidden within you. At first, your faith was weak, scrawny even, so I had full control over you. But then…"

It hesitated. "…your faith grew."

I watched as two other words, "No" and "More," suddenly stepped into the conversation. Delay groaned. "At first, I resisted them. I like lingering. I enjoy doing nothing. But 'No' and 'More' were relentless. They kept pressing into me, forcing me into alignment. Annoying little things."

I gasped as I realized what was happening. Delay had been overthrown. "No More Delay" had been formed — a declaration birthed by faith!

"We stand together now," the words said in unison, "and we have one assignment: To bring about change. Use us. Speak us out. Send us into the atmosphere, and we will remove every obstacle standing in your way."

The Word of God Moves

God led me to Ezekiel 12:28 (GNT): "So tell them, this is what the Sovereign Lord says: None of My words will be delayed any longer; whatever I say will be fulfilled."

Then, the words "No More Delay" spoke again. "Release us."

"Speak us out, and we will accomplish what God has assigned. His Word cannot be postponed."

At that moment, something exploded inside me.

I didn't even realize I had moved, but suddenly, I was on the floor — laid out, full of anointing and courage. And then ... I laughed. Not just a soft chuckle. I laughed hard. I laughed so loud that my stomach ached. It was the laughter of breakthrough. The laughter of freedom. The laughter of knowing something powerful had just been released in my life.

Sending the Word into the Future

I stood up with no hesitation, no fear. Immediately, I sent "No More Delay" into the earth.

"NO MORE DELAY!" I declared. "Go now into my future! Knock down every obstacle in my life. Do the same for anyone connected to me. NO MORE DELAY in my ministry! NO MORE DELAY in the release of my book! NO MORE DELAY in my business! NO MORE DELAY in the increase of my wealth and finances. NO MORE DELAY in my divine health and healing. NO MORE DELAY in the divine connections I need to help me fulfill destiny! CRUSH every barrier keeping my destiny partners from finding me! NO MORE DELAY! NO MORE DELAY! NO MORE DELAY! NO MORE DELAY! NO MORE DELAY!

I watched in awe as "No More Delay" shot out of the window — faster than the speed of light, disappearing into my future to accomplish all that I had commanded.

Then, I heard it. A soft voice. "Your time has come."

The Word is Alive

God had given me a revelation of the power of my words.

Hebrews 4:12 says, "The Word of God, you see, is alive and moving" (Voice).

And I had just witnessed it firsthand. God's Word is not idle, not static — it is alive. It is waiting for us to release it. Mark 11:24 reminds us: "You can pray for anything, and if you believe that you've received it, it will be yours" (NLT). Words, when connected to faith, create realities.

The Word of God is a living, breathing force, designed to accomplish His will and bring His promises to pass. Isaiah

55:11 confirms it: "So is my word that goes out from my mouth: It will not return to me empty but will accomplish what I desire and achieve the purpose for which I sent it" (NIV).

No More Delay. Not tomorrow. Not next year. Not when it's convenient.

The time is now.

Your Turn: Speak the Word

As I share this encounter with you, I feel led to proclaim that your faith is intensifying right now. Your faith is forging an alliance with the Word of God to transport heaven's dreams into your life. Will you allow your faith to establish a relationship with the Word abiding in you?

Take a moment to reflect:

- What areas of your life feel delayed or stuck?
- What words of faith can you speak over those areas today?

Just as I declared "No More Delay," you too can send forth words of faith to transform your realities. Decide where your words will go and send them forth! Speak to the delays, the obstacles, and the barriers. Command them to move in Jesus' name.

Remember, your words have power. When aligned with God's Word and fueled by faith, they become unstoppable forces of change. So, laugh with joy, rise with courage, and speak with confidence. Your time has come.

NO MORE DELAY.

Reflection Questions

1. What does "No More Delay" mean to you in this season of your life?

2. How can you use the power of your words to align with God's promises?

3. What step of faith can you take today to activate the Word of God in your life?

The Power of Confessions

The tongue can speak words that bring life or death. Those who love to talk must be ready to accept what it brings.
— Proverbs 18:21 (TPT)

The Power of Confession

Faith-filled words (what Christians call confessions) are more than just words. They are powerful declarations that shape our thoughts, realities, and very existence.

Just as our Father spoke the universe into existence, our words have the power to create, transform, and align our lives with God's promises. I didn't always understand the magnitude of this truth until one extraordinary encounter with God changed everything.

An Encounter with the Creator

One day, I was in my room, reading the Book of Genesis, when I felt the Holy Spirit's presence fill the air around me.

Then, I heard it — a familiar, loving whisper.

"Hello, sweetie."

Excitement bubbled up inside me.

"Hello, Daddy! What's going on?"

His tone was playful. *"Close your eyes. I'm going to take you to the beginning. I want to show you how I created man — beyond just what you've read in Genesis. It's a good book, right?"*

I chuckled inwardly. Show off! You know it's good.

As if reading my thoughts, I heard the sound of His laughter fill my ears.

"Close your eyes," He repeated. *"Let's go."*

With a joyful chuckle, I obeyed.

Witnessing Creation Unfold

Suddenly, I stood on solid ground, flanked by the Father, the Son, and the Holy Spirit. Before us, was what looked like a vast, untouched canvas — an endless expanse of divine potential. I believe that the greatest artists envision their creations long before the brush meets canvas.

God was no different.

Though the space before us seemed empty, I could feel the anticipation, the excitement, the love radiating from Him. Hours seemed to pass as God contemplated His greatest masterpiece. Unlike everything else He had created; this would be different.

This would be His image.

His hands reached for mine, and like a loving father introducing His child to something sacred, He placed my palm against His chest. His heartbeat thundered beneath my fingers, steady and strong. I closed my eyes, completely engulfed by His love.

And then, all creation responded.

The ground trembled, volcanoes erupted, clouds burst forth with rain, ocean waves rose and danced, the sun shone its brightest, rocks leapt from the earth, flowers bloomed in bursts of color, tree leaves shook with life.

All of creation was praising God, reciting in unison: *"Son of God, come forth!"* (Romans 8:19)

Even the angels stood in silent wonder, watching as God prepared to reveal His greatest design.

The Birth of Adam

Genesis 2:7 says, "The Lord God formed man from the dust of the ground and breathed into his nostrils the breath of life; and man became a living soul." But what I saw went beyond those words.

The Father, Son, and Holy Spirit spoke as one voice, one mind, one thought: *"Let Us make man in Our image."*

A heavenly choir erupted in praise: "Glory to God!"

Then, God's hands appeared. Like a master sculptor, He moved with deliberate, tender precision. He smiled as He worked — drawing, painting, chiseling, shaping, molding, and placing. From nothing, a form appeared in the dust.

I watched as the weight of God's love intensified. My knees buckled under the sheer power of His affection. He glanced at me, placed a gentle kiss on my cheek, and suddenly, I was strengthened. For a moment, time seemed to stand still.

God gazed at the form before Him — not with haste, but with intentionality, devotion, and deep love.

Jesus stepped forward. *"Let Me do it,"* He said.

The Holy Spirit playfully pouted. *"Aww, I wanted to do it!"*

And then, as one complete being, they moved in unity. With the tenderness of a father, God lifted the lifeless form into His arms. Then, He breathed. A whirlwind of divine breath filled the being's chest. His belly rose and fell as he inhaled the very essence of God. With everything in Him, God exhaled. The being inhaled. Over and over, an exchange of life, an exchange of oneness.

Until —

The man gasped his first breath.

God cradled him close and whispered: *"I call you Adam."*

Tears streamed from God's eyes, falling onto Adam's face like rain. And then — Adam's eyes opened. For the first time, creation met its Creator.

God gazed at him with pure, unshakable love and spoke one word: *"Son."*

A breath later, Adam responded. His first word ever spoken, filled with awe and reverence: *"Father."*

Tears streamed down my face. For the first time, I truly understood what love was.

The Power of Your Words

What separates us from the rest of creation is God's breath within us — His very life, His voice, His power. All that God is, was in that one breath. Unlike the animals, we were created in His image, designed to speak as He speaks.

"Death and life are in the power of the tongue" (Proverbs 18:21).

Adam's first word was 'Father.' What will be your first word? What will you speak into existence? Because your words create. What reality will your confessions shape?

Prayer and Declarations

Choose Joy

Scripture:
James 1:2-4 (Voice)
"Don't run from tests and hardships, brothers and sisters. As difficult as they are, you will ultimately find joy in them; if you embrace them, your faith will blossom under pressure and teach you true patience as you endure. And true patience brought on by endurance will equip you to complete the long journey and cross the finish line — mature, complete, and wanting nothing."

Prayer and Declaration:
I declare that I cross the finish line daily. I blossom under pressure and WIN! I embrace my trials and find true patience to endure, building up my godly character. Therefore, in the midst of everything, I CHOOSE JOY! I am mature, I am complete, and I want nothing.

Action Step: Shout "JESUS!" and laugh out loud seven times. Watch your attitude shift as joy fills your heart.

Days of Laughter

Scripture:
Psalm 30:4-5 (Message Translation)
"Sing your hearts out to God! Thank Him to His face! He gets angry occasionally, but across a lifetime, there is only love.

The nights of crying your eyes out give way to days of laughter."

Prayer and Declaration:
I declare and decree that I receive joy in the morning. I am saturated with laughter for days and permeated with everlasting joy. Though I may have cried my eyes out, my days are now filled with laughter. My praise makes room for a lifetime of LOVE and the benefits of my God.

Medical Laughter

Scripture:
Proverbs 17:22 (God's Word Translation)
"A joyful heart is good medicine, but depression drains one's strength."

Prayer and Declaration:

I declare and decree that I have a joyful heart, and laughter is my daily dose of medicine. It frees me from all depression, viruses, ailments, and dis-eases. When I laugh, walls of despair and bad health tumble down. My body experiences good health and healing in the name of Jesus.

Laugh at Your Past

Scripture:
Nehemiah 8:10 (Voice)
"This day is special. It is sacred to our Lord. Do not grieve over your past mistakes. Let the Eternal's own joy be your protection!"

Prayer and Declaration:
I declare and decree that God's own joy protects me from the devil and his evil schemes. Today is the day the Lord has made, and I am supernaturally infused with God's strength and joy. I celebrate and laugh at my past mistakes, watching them be exterminated.

Laugh in Relief

Scripture:
Job 5:22 (KJV)
"At destruction and famine, thou shalt laugh: neither shalt thou be afraid of the beasts of the earth."

Prayer and Declaration:
I declare and decree that I laugh in the midst of destruction. When the Lord laughs, He confuses my enemies, causing them to turn against each other and experience famine. Every plot they prepared for me, may my enemies experience the negative effects of their own plans. I laugh at destruction in

the name of Jesus! (Physically laugh several times.) I am not afraid of the enemy, and I declare that I am free.

Final Encouragement

Joy and laughter are not simple emotions — they are weapons of warfare, declarations of faith, and expressions of God's presence in our lives. As you meditate on these scriptures and speak these declarations, remember that your joy is rooted in the unchanging nature of God. No matter what you face, you can choose joy, laugh at the enemy's schemes, and walk in the freedom and victory Christ has already secured for you.

So, laugh out loud, shout His name, and let your joy be a testimony of His goodness. Your days of laughter are here.

Laughter Quotes

- "The human race has one really effective weapon, and that is laughter." — Mark Twain

- "The person who can bring the spirit of laughter into a room is indeed blessed." — Benett Cerf

- "Earth laughs in flowers." — Ralph Waldo Emerson

- "The greatest prayer you could ever pray is to laugh every day." — Unknown

- "It is cheerful to God when you rejoice or laugh from the bottom of your heart." — Martin Luther King Jr.
- "If we couldn't laugh, we would all go insane." — Robert Frost
- "Laughter is poison to fear." — George R.R. Martin
- "There is nothing in the world so irresistibly contagious as laughter and good humor." — Unknown
- "Sometimes I laugh so hard the tears run down my leg." — Unknown

- "God is a comedian playing to an audience too afraid to laugh." — Voltaire

- "Cancer is probably not the funniest thing in the world, but I'm a comedian, and even cancer couldn't stop me from seeing the humor in what I went through." — Gilda Radner

- "I have not seen anyone dying of laughter, but I know millions who are dying because they are not laughing." — Dr. Madan Kataria

About the Author

Dr. Nandi Louise, affectionately known as the Laughter Transformation Strategist, is a Certified Laughter Leader with the World Laughter Tour and the visionary founder of *Laughter to the Nations*. As a laughaholic, laughpreneur, laughter strategist, and self-proclaimed joyologist, Nandi leads with the conviction that laughter is not just joy or entertainment — it's healing, it's medicine, and it's ministry.

Her anointed calling is to help people access the transformative power of laughter for spiritual, mental, and physical healing. Nandi believes that when people feel whole and worthy, they are more capable of meeting life's challenges with clarity, purpose, and intention.

With a degree in Psychology and over 15 years of experience as an at-risk youth counselor, Nandi has always had a deep passion for empowering young people to discover their worth and walk confidently in their purpose. Her work in youth advocacy reflects the same compassion, resilience, and faith that infuse her laughter ministry. Recently, she was nominated for an honorary doctorate degree in humanitarian service, recognizing her impactful contributions to communities and individuals, alike.

From a young age, Nandi Louise has used laughter as a powerful tool to rise above personal trials and strengthen her walk with God. Now, as a motivational speaker, laughter wellness coach, and certified laughter facilitator, she teaches others to do the same. Through dynamic seminars, coaching sessions, and national speaking engagements, she equips individuals and communities to conquer life with God — one joyful breath at a time.

Her ministry, *Laughter to the Nations*, is a transformational outreach that promotes holistic well-being through the gift of laughter. Rooted in faith and driven by compassion, Nandi's work goes beyond surface smiles. She empowers others to use laughter as a spiritual tool to ground themselves intentionally, overcome adversity, and find divine joy in the everyday.

Recognized as a trailblazer in the field of laughter wellness, Dr. Nandi Louise continues to shine light into the lives of others, forging new paths toward wholeness, purpose, and peace. With her contagious joy and unwavering faith, she is on a mission to create a world where laughter is not only cherished, but celebrated, as a sacred pathway to healing, connection, and fulfillment.

www.ingramcontent.com/pod-product-compliance
Lightning Source LLC
Chambersburg PA
CBHW031249290426
44109CB00012B/494